I'LL BE YOUR LIGHT

YOU HAVE TO BE STRONG
TO SURVIVE

MANNIE VENENO

ARCHWAY
PUBLISHING

Archway Publishing books may be ordered
through booksellers or by contacting:

Archway Publishing
1663 Liberty Drive
Bloomington, IN 47403
www.archwaypublishing.com
844-669-3957

Because of the dynamic nature of the Internet, any web addresses or
links contained in this book may have changed since publication and
may no longer be valid. The views expressed in this work are solely those
of the author and do not necessarily reflect the views of the publisher,
and the publisher hereby disclaims any responsibility for them.

Any people depicted in stock imagery provided by Getty Images are
models, and such images are being used for illustrative purposes only.
Certain stock imagery © Getty Images.

ISBN: 978-1-6657-2094-6 (sc)
ISBN: 978-1-6657-2093-9 (hc)
ISBN: 978-1-6657-2095-3 (e)

Library of Congress Control Number: 2022907753

Print information available on the last page.

Archway Publishing rev. date: 04/20/2022

CONTENTS

INTRODUCTION

THIRTY-THREE YEARS IN THE DARK. That's enough to push anyone over the edge, to succumb to the pain and loneliness, to want to turn around and take it out on the world. But if there's one thing the darkness has taught me, it is that there are always choices, and you have to choose. Do you continue on the path and spread the darkness like a virus, infecting one and then others exponentially? Or do you run toward that small pinpoint of light in the distance, embracing it until it becomes part of you and then reflecting it, so the world gets brighter and brighter? That's the choice I made, but I won't lie—it hasn't been easy. I'm Mannie Veneno, and this is my story, a story of abuse, violence, poverty, and shame. This is the darkness I grew up in and the reason I run to the light today. This is my struggle to overcome, and I hope it will shine like a beacon for others fighting to get out of the dark. Growing up, I felt all alone. I had a dad who abused us and a mom who didn't have the courage to walk away. I didn't have any role models to look up to. Everyone around me was in gangs and into crime, drinking, and doing drugs, and I didn't see any other clear path forward. What I did know was I didn't want to be like them.

The gift of this seemingly unfortunate life is that relatively early on in life, I found that small, unbreakable part of myself that pushed me to keep going, to do better, to survive. As a kid, I hardly watched TV. All I did was focus on myself and how to better myself through every stage of pain and darkness I went through. That's how I survived, because the fire inside me was stronger than the fire around me. Then one day, everything started to change. I met good people, people who loved me and cared for me, people who made me forget about my problems and start to see solutions instead. They brought out the best in me and made me want to be better and spread love to the world, instead of hate. They taught me that it doesn't matter how much money you have; it is about the difference you make in people's lives. That is what I hope to do with this book. I want to change your life. I want to give you hope. I want you to know that you're not alone, that someone cares for you, and that you will get through the darkness. I want you to realize your strength and your ability to create the life you want with it. It is easy to hate the world for what has happened to you, but life gets so much better when you start to love instead. When you stand against darkness, master it within yourself, and do not lose your faith and love for humankind, you will no longer be a survivor but a warrior like me. I hope you enjoy my story.

1

THE CYCLE BEGINS

MY MOTHER, FIAZA, COMES FROM a very poor background. She lived with her brother, Javed, and sister, Zenath, at their father's house in Jalalpur, Pakistan. Their home was an hour away from their mother, who lived at her parents' house with her brother and family in Sialkot. My grandma wanted to see Fiaza, Javed, and Zenath, so she told my great-grandmother to bring them for a visit, and she did. Someone in their neighborhood told my grandma's brother Toffal that kids had been dropped off at his house, and he was enraged by the news. Toffal came rushing home looking for his sister (my grandma) to talk to her. My grandma was hanging up clothes to dry on the roof. In anger, Toffal rushed upstairs and started arguing and yelling at my grandma because his wife didn't like kids at her house. He then grabbed a spear and started beating my grandma with the dull side, asking, "Why did you tell

Mom to bring the kids here? You can eat bread made of gold, but I don't want the kids here." My grandma didn't say a word because she was so scared and distraught. Toffal ignored her and went downstairs to talk to my great-grandma. "Take those kids back however you brought them here," he told her.

My great-grandma couldn't do or say anything because her son had serious anger issues. My grandma started getting the kids ready so they could be sent back home to her dad's house. She was crying the whole time because she had barely gotten to spend any time with them before my great-grandma was forced to take my mom and her siblings back to their dad's house. My mom and her siblings were sobbing because they wanted to stay with their mom. On the way back to Jalalpur, my mom and her siblings cried the entire trip. My great-grandma, while teary-eyed, tried to calm the kids down, telling them, "It's OK! Your mom will come see you soon." But my mom and her siblings would not stop crying because they didn't want to stay at their dad's house alone. When they got back to their dad's house, my mom's brother, Javed, started bashing his head against the wall, to the point where his nose started bleeding, because he didn't like being with his dad. "Please stop. Don't cry. Your mom will be here soon enough," my great-grandma said to Javed.

My mom's grandpa lived with her dad, and a month after this incident, my mom's dad took Javed to Lahore and left my mom and Zenath at home with their grandpa, who was eighty years old.

Her grandpa had them stay downstairs. There was no door and no glass on the windows. Anyone and anything could've come inside. Her grandpa would stay and sleep on the roof, leaving my mom and Zenath downstairs. One night, Zenath and my mom were sleeping downstairs when suddenly eight to ten dogs came into the house and started barking aggressively at them. They started crying out of fear for their lives. After they sobbed for a bit, the dogs got tired and ended up leaving them alone. After they left, my mom and Zenath got up to walk outside through the neighborhood to look for shelter while it was pouring rain. No one opened the door for them, so they walked back toward their house and saw their neighbor Thimi's house. They sat down on her porch, crying, hoping they would let them in. Finally, Thimi's mom noticed Zenath and my mom. "I think that's Afzal's (my mom's dad) daughters," said Thimi's mom. She came down and opened the door for them and let them sleep inside their house. That same night, while it was raining, my mom's grandpa went down the stairs, slipped, and fell, breaking his pelvis bone. Thimi's mom said to Fiaza, "Allah (the god) punished him for leaving you downstairs alone like that."

At this time, Fiaza's mom, my grandma, was in Sialkot. She prayed to God, "Please let me have my kids," for three months straight while starving herself. Every day since she started praying, her mom would cook food and take it to her to eat. My grandma would not eat.

"I don't want food. I want my kids," said my grandma one evening.

"Honey, you know how Toffal is. How can I bring your kids?" my great-grandma responded.

"I don't know. I just want my kids," said my grandma.

My great-grandma got up and left the room. The next day, my grandma went into the main room where Toffal and his wife, mom, and dad were. She told them, "I don't want to eat bread made of gold. I just want my kids."

"If you leave this house to go to your kids, you won't be coming back inside our house," said Toffal.

"That's fine with me. I won't come back," said my grandma. She went upstairs and started packing her clothes.

Then my great-grandma walked in and asked, "Are you sure you want to do this?"

My grandma responded, "Yes, I want to see my kids, and I don't care if my husband beats me or not."

My great-grandmother started to help my grandma pack her things.

Back in Jalalpur, my mother, Javed, and Zenath were outside playing. They got hungry, so my mom went around asking for food. She found a lady in the neighborhood who was willing to spare some food. She gave them one piece of roti (bread). My mom went back with the roti and split it between Javed and Zenath.

A bit later, my great-grandma came to Jalalpur with my grandma to drop her off with her kids. When my grandma saw her kids, they were a complete mess. Their clothes were torn, their hair was dirty with lice, and they looked malnourished. My grandma couldn't help but cry when she saw them. "I don't want to stay here. Take me with you," my grandma said to her mom.

"No, no, you know I can't do that. You know how Toffal will be," said my great-grandma.

My grandma just stood there in silence.

"I'll come visit you in a month to see how you're doing," said my great-grandma to her daughter. So my grandma parted ways with her mom.

At this point, my grandma had no choice but to go back to her abusive husband. For three weeks straight, it was back to fighting and throwing each other's dishes. A month later, my great-grandma came back to check up on her daughter and her kids.

When my grandma saw her, she just broke down, crying her eyes out. "I don't want to stay here. This man is crazy! He beats me and my children and never gives us any food or drink. I'm forced to go outside and beg for food just to feed my kids. Please just take me somewhere."

"OK, get everyone ready, and I'll take you somewhere." My great-grandmother got her daughter and all of her grandchildren on the bus and took the kids somewhere in Sialkot. She couldn't take them home because she didn't want her son to throw a fit again. Instead, she went to the house of an old friend and asked, "Is a room available for my daughter and her kids?"

"The door is always open for you. You can come any time," said her friend.

She left Mom, Javed, and Zenath at her friend's house and went back home before Toffal noticed she was gone. My great-grandma went to her friend's house to check up on my mom and her siblings and then went back and forth to Toffal and her family's house for six months straight. She also gave my grandma money for food and drink.

Sometime later, my great-grandma told her daughter that Toffal found out what she'd been doing and was looking for her like a madman. She told her she needed to get out of there and go somewhere. So my grandma got Fiaza and her siblings ready early in the morning. She was a lone woman with three kids in a fucked-up world. She had nowhere to go. She had no choice but to go back to her abusive husband in Jalalpur, so she got on a bus with her children and went back. When she got there, her abusive father was nowhere to be found. She found some of his family, and they told her, "He moved to Lahore a little while ago." At a loss for words, she assumed where her husband would be, at his sister Neese's house.

2

NEGLECTED IN LAHORE

MY GRANDMA WAS FORCED TO catch another bus and traveled to Lahore with her children. They got off the bus and found a rickshaw. Once at her husband's sister's house, she got out and knocked. His sister came out, and my grandma asked if her husband was here. "No, he's not here. He is a couple of blocks down over there." My grandma went inside. Neese started cooking food for them, and they all ate together.

My grandma asked Neese, "Where is my husband living right now?" Neese offered to take them to her brother's house. "Yes, please. Let's go," my grandma responded.

My grandma arrived at her husband's house in Lahore and knocked on the door. No one answered, so they assumed no one was home. My grandma then went to a neighbor's to hang out there until her husband came back. A few hours later, he came back and saw his sister outside. My grandma came out with her kids, along with Neese. My grandma's husband got enraged. "I don't want you to stay here with me. I don't have money to feed you."

"Don't do this. They're your kids," Neese said to her brother.

The townspeople heard everything that was being said. They all came together and had a small protest, telling my grandma's husband, "They are just kids! You have to let them in. She has little kids with her and nowhere else to go, nothing to eat! Let her in!"

He was forced to listen and let them inside. For three whole days, my mom, Zenath, and Javed asked for food to eat. My mom's dad was cooking food for himself, and he ran out of masala (spices), so he asked my mom to go get some from the store.

"I don't want to go. Give me one rupee, and then I'll go get it!" said my mom playfully as she walked outside to go play with the neighborhood kids. My mom's dad went to see if she had left yet and saw she hadn't. He grabbed her by the hair and dragged her across the ground, smacking her in the face while they were still outside.

"Are you going to go get the masala I need or not?" said my mom's dad.

"Yes, I'll go get it," said my mom. She went and got the masala and came back with it. He finished cooking the food. He made himself a plate and then went out so he could head to work. My mom went to check the pot for some food, only to see there was no food left. He went to work with all the food and didn't leave his wife and his kids food. He did the same thing for the majority of their time staying there. He never gave them any spare food and always got angry, starting arguments and beating and yelling at my grandma and her kids. Every time my grandma's husband cooked food, he left and took all the food.

While he was out working, my mom went over to the pantry to see if her mom could make some roti. She noticed two big handprints in the flour and lost all hope of getting food. My mom's dad would put his hands in the flour to leave his handprints in it, just to make sure no one touched his food. He did not want my grandma to use his cooking supplies to feed herself and her kids. So my grandma started going outside and asking everyone in the neighborhood for food so she could feed her kids. Then one day my grandma got tired of asking for food, so she asked her little brother Parvez for some money to get a sewing machine. Instead of giving her money, he went to Kuwait and bought her a sewing machine. Then my grandma started sewing clothes for money, taking her kids along with her. She found a factory that sold peanuts, and she worked there along with her kids so she could make more money when her sewing business was slow.

There was a friend in the neighborhood who made toffee candy at home, and my grandma would go pick them up and give them to her kids so they could help wrap each piece of candy. There would be work for them one week, then no work the next week. When there was no work, my mom and her siblings asked her dad for food, but he never gave it to them. They prayed every day and every night that someone in the neighborhood would give them food. There was only one neighbor who would give my grandma and her kids food in the afternoon.

One day, my mom asked her dad for food. He started name-calling, arguing, and refusing to give them anything because he claimed to have no money. My grandma got the townspeople again to help persuade him. Then he agreed and said, "Fine, I will give them five rupees every day. He then gave them five rupees for the next four days. One of those days, he gave my grandma five rupees and an extra five rupees the same day. He told her, "Hold onto this for me. I'll grab it in the morning." So my grandma took the extra five rupees and told my mom to put it on the shelf.

The next day, my grandpa asked for the five rupees back, so my grandma told my mom to bring the money she had given her the night before. My mom brought the money and handed it to her mom. Her mom gave it to her husband, and he noticed it was one rupee short. He then started a big fight, involving yelling, hitting, and threatening. He said to his wife, "I'm gonna sell your scissors to make it a full five rupees."

My grandma told her daughter (my mom), "Check behind the things in the closet. Maybe you dropped it." My mom went and checked and found that one rupee had fallen behind the suitcase when my mom was putting it away. My mom brought the rupee back to her dad, and he walked out without saying a word.

After four days of giving my grandma five rupees, he just stopped. The next day, my grandma asked my mom to go ask for the money again. "I don't have it," said my mom's dad, and he started yelling and spouting disgusting comments. My grandma got mad and went next door to her neighbors' house to let her know what was happening. The neighbor told her that they would talk tomorrow with the townspeople.

The next day came around, and she got all the people together, and everyone was commenting on the situation. "You have such small kids. If you're not giving them food, where will they get it from?" said the townspeople to my grandpa.

He then told my grandma, "Go get money from your mom and dad."

The townspeople then said, "Why should she get it from her mom and dad? They are your kids, your wife."

My grandma's husband replied, "She's not my wife," abruptly disowning the relationship.

My grandma stayed there for two weeks. Then one day my grandpa came downstairs to talk to his wife. He said, "I have a friend, and he wants me to come over for dinner with the family." He took his wife, Javed, Zenath, and Fiaza to the friend's house. They had my grandma and her kids sit in a separate room while my grandpa talked to his friend. Fiaza's mom was starting to feel impatient because they were taking a really long time to talk. My grandma cracked the door to see what they were doing, and she overheard her husband talking about selling her and the kids. She went out of the room and told her husband and his friend that the kids needed to use the bathroom, which was outside.

They said, "OK. Come back when you're done." So she took the kids and ran as soon as she stepped outside of the house. She took trains, got rides, and asked for help from other people. She also looked for someone who could rent a room to her. After looking for two to three days, she found an old friend in Lahore who was willing to help. However, they didn't have room for my grandma and her kids. My grandma begged her to help her.

Out of remorse, she told my grandma, "I have a small storage room. I can clean that up, and you all can stay there." The storage room was the size of a queen-size bed. After a few months, my grandpa found out where my grandma was hiding. He went there one to two times a week, but the family wouldn't let him come inside.

One day the family let my grandpa inside, and he got a chance to talk to his wife. "I'm sorry. I won't do this anymore. Can you come home now?" my grandpa said. Every time, he came, my grandma refused.

The family my grandma was staying with had a son who would talk to my mom and her siblings. His mom did not like that one bit. The mom of the family told my grandma to clean that room and leave her house.

Then my grandma got tired of living this way. She went to her parents' house in Sialkot for shelter. My great-grandma and her husband didn't want my grandma and her kids to stay there. They got my grandma and her kids in the car and took them back to Lahore with my grandma's husband. "That's your house. You chose to go back to your husband. That's your house now, so you can go back over there. Once you go back, I will give you some money for food and drinks for you and your children," said my great-grandpa. My grandma was scared of her dad, so she just agreed.

After being dropped off in Lahore at her husband's house, my grandma went to her parents' house with her kids to get money every month. That way, her kids could go out and not have to be with their dad. Then they would come back to Lahore. She did this for about a year. While they stayed with my grandpa, Javed always went outside from the afternoon to after midnight. He would hang out and walk everywhere with his friends and watch movies. Javed's mom didn't like that. My grandma took Javed and her other kids to her dad's house. "He always goes out and never comes home. If he stays there, he'll become corrupt. Can you take him in and care for him here?" asked my grandma.

"Yes, that's fine. He can stay here." Javed didn't want to stay there, but my grandma was forced to leave him there so he could live a better life.

My mom saw her brother was staying with her grandma and grandpa. "I want to stay here with Grandma too!" said my mom. So my grandma dropped my mom off at my great-grandma's house. A month went by, and my grandma came back to get more money. Then my mom went back to Lahore with her.

3

SHELTER IN SIALKOT

MY GRANDPA DIDN'T LIKE THE fact that he had people living with him. He told my grandma that she should go back to her parents' house and he would help her whenever she needed money. "I'll come check on you when you need money, and I'll drop it off for you." My grandma agreed. My grandpa then drove my grandma and her kids to my great-grandpa's house, which also had a furniture store downstairs, and dropped them off. After he dropped them off, they never heard from him again, nor did he send any money to my grandma.

After getting to the furniture store, my great-grandma had my grandma and her kids follow her, so she could walk them to Parvez's house. Parvez lived ten minutes away from the furniture store with his wife, Suraiya, and their kids. Parvez had a house where he stayed with Suraiya and another guesthouse right next to his house. Parvez was completely fine with my grandma staying there. My mom and her siblings got really excited because they were finally staying somewhere that didn't have someone yelling and beating them every other day.

At the time, Parvez was on vacation for three months. When his vacation was over, he had to go back to Kuwait for work for about a year. My grandma and her kids stayed there for about a year. Parvez would go to Kuwait and back to Sialkot every year, which was four hours away. One day, he came back with a surprise for Javed. It was a passport so Javed could go to Kuwait with him. Parvez took Javed to the National Database and Registration Authority (NADRA) to get a photo for his passport. Javed went into the office with Parvez, but one of the people could tell he was too young, and he couldn't make the ID for him. Javed and Parvez had no choice but to go home and come back the next day. Javed used some makeup to draw a mustache on him to make him look a bit older. Parvez then took Javed back to the NADRA. There were different workers there, so getting his ID and passport was no problem at all. Javed went to Kuwait with Parvez and stayed there with him. When Javed came to Sialkot, Parvez stayed in Kuwait. They would alternate.

Five years later, Javed came back by himself with gifts and souvenirs for my mom and her sister. Javed went into the house where my grandma and her kids were staying to meet Suraiya, but she had left out of the back door to avoid seeing him. Javed got sad and went to his mom, crying because Suraiya didn't want to see him, even after five years. She truly didn't like them at all.

Javed stayed with his mom and his siblings for the next three months. They all had a good time. Then Javed went back to Kuwait. Some time after that, Parvez got enough time for a vacation, so he came back to Sialkot to be with his wife.

Some time had passed, and Parvez's wife, Suraiya, had gotten tired of seeing my grandma and her kids there. "You have to kick them out of the house. I don't want them here," said Suraiya.

"I will kick you out, but I'm not kicking my sister out," Parvez responded. Then Suraiya got sad and went to her parents' house.

Sometime after that, Parvez's vacation was over. He had to go back to Kuwait for his work. While Parvez was in Kuwait, his wife, Suraiya, came back and started doing witchcraft in the middle of the night. She was desperate to get my grandma and her kids out of her husband's house.

Suraiya then made a makeshift stove out of mud, wrote something in a few eggs, set the eggs in the middle of the stove, and covered it with mud. My grandma woke my mom up and told her, "Whether you believe it or not, she was definitely doing something last night."

My mom replied, "No, Mom, she was probably just making something to eat. I'll check the stove." When the sun came up, my mom went and broke the stove made from mud in the middle and found four eggs. My mom opened the eggs up and saw demonic-like lettering. She realized what my grandma was saying was true. That same day, Suraiya went to a neighbor's house and started talking smack about my grandma and her kids, because my grandma would not leave.

When my grandma saw the eggs my mom took to her, she went out to the neighborhood and told the townspeople, "Suraiya wanted us out of her house so badly she had the nerve to do witchcraft on me and my kids!" Word got around, and the next day, the same neighbor went to Parvez's house where my grandma and mom were staying. She started telling Suraiya everything that had been said about her, from the stove being broken and the eggs having demonic lettering to the witchcraft on them. When Suraiya heard that, she got enraged and started a huge fight between my grandma and her kids.

She falsely accused my grandma of stealing clothes. My great-grandpa came over that same day and was told what was going on. But he knew she was lying. "Whatever clothes got stolen, give me a piece of the fabric, and I'll get the same exact matching design," said my great-grandpa. Suraiya didn't have anything to say. My great-grandpa ended up leaving after that. Every day after that, Suraiya used every excuse in the book to start a fight between my grandma and her kids.

Then one day Suraiya's daughter's watch went missing. Without a doubt, she automatically assumed it was my grandma and her kids. A few hours later, Suraiya's daughter found the watch on the staircase on Suraiya's side of the house; she lived in a guesthouse right next to the main house. Suraiya responded, "They probably took it and threw it right there." My grandma and her kids were blamed for all kinds of things, but they couldn't say anything because they were staying in her house. All they could do was stand by and listen. My mom helped take care of Suraiya's kids and cleaned up the house like a maid, yet that still didn't make her happy.

After three months, Parvez went back to Kuwait. Two to three months passed, and my grandma noticed Suraiya was pregnant. When she was about six months pregnant, a stranger snuck into Suraiya's house at two in the morning, stabbed her in the stomach, and ran off. All the houses in the neighborhood were very close together. She started screaming so loudly everyone in the neighborhood heard her. They all came running to see what had happened. One of the neighbors rushed her to the hospital. They bandaged her up, and the doctors found the baby had been stabbed also. So they were forced to take the baby out and operate on her and Suraiya. Thankfully, the baby ended up being OK. When the news got out, Parvez came back to see if everything was all right. Once he saw everything was OK, he had to head back to work because he hadn't gotten a break. Two to three days after staying with Suraiya, Parvez left for Kuwait.

A few months later when Suraiya got better, she started doing witchcraft again. She hated my grandma and her kids so much she went to great lengths to do whatever she could to get rid of them. As life went on, my grandma wanted to arrange a marriage for her daughter, Zenath. A few families came to the house to talk about the marriage. There was one mom and dad who liked Zenath a lot. Then my grandma went to their house to choose a man she liked for Zenath. My grandma thought, *Maybe if I get my daughters married at a young age, they will be taken care of better than I can care for them.* After that was done, my grandma came home.

The family who liked Zenath came over a couple times a week, just to see Zenath, talk to her, and get to know her better. One month later, Parvez got a vacation from his work, so he came back to Sialkot. It was nighttime when Parvez got home. Suraiya was eager to vent to him and tell him every bad thing that had happened while he was gone. She stayed up all night telling him about everything, making up lies. She lied and said a bunch of random men were coming to the house, and her daughter was getting older, and it was not safe. Suraiya even blamed the stabbing on my grandma, explaining she hired someone to do it. Parvez was just speechless. He actually believed Suraiya and didn't question a word.

The day after, Parvez called my grandma to say, "I can't have you stay here any longer, so I'm going to need you to pack your stuff, clean the house, and get out." My grandma had no choice but to listen because it wasn't her place to say anything. After my grandma and her kids left Parvez's house, she desperately looked for a place to stay. Thankfully, she found a family willing to rent a room in the same neighborhood. She stayed there for about a month.

The husband of the family's house was nicknamed Sha. While they were staying there, the family my grandma met for Zenath's marriage came to Sha's house to arrange the marriage. They got married right at the house. Zenath then had to leave with her husband to his family's house. A few days later, Sha received a phone call from his friend, who was soon to be my dad, telling Sha he was in trouble and he needed to come pick him up as soon as possible. Sha went out to get his friend and brought him to his house.

One day, my mom had a dream where she was completely surrounded by water. Then she saw her friend and asked her, "Where's Chami's (another friend's) house?" Her friend stood up and pointed in the direction of her house. When my mom looked where she was pointing, she saw hundreds of small graves around her. Then in the middle, Chami's grave was the biggest one there. When my mom saw Chami's grave, she said to her friend, "No, I'm OK. Chami's house is too far. I'll go next time." Then my mom woke up.

The next morning, my mom went to her neighbor's house to wash clothes. The neighbor told my mom before washing her clothes that the washing machines gave off a lot of electricity. So my mom's neighbor explained how to use the washer. "You have to unplug the machine, put water in, load your clothes in, *then* plug the machine in and start washing." After she finished explaining that to my mom, she did three baskets of laundry, and then she was on her last round of clothes. My mom had her bare feet in the water on the floor and was putting water into the machine with a metal bucket. When she filled up the bucket the second time, her neighbor's daughter, who was my mom's friend, plugged the washing machine in while my mom was pouring the water into the machine, holding a metal bucket, with her feet in the water. My mom got electrocuted and was stuck there. My mom's friend unplugged the machine and got my mom back to normal, but she was still in shock. Then her friend came into the room laughing. My mom was pretty mad, but the dream she had made her think, *Maybe if I went to Chami's grave, that wouldn't have happened.*

4

THE CYCLE REPEATS

THE NEXT DAY, SOMEONE WAS knocking on the door, but no one was answering. My grandma had gone to get groceries, and my mom's sisters were at school. No one was home besides my dad and my mom. My mom didn't want to open the door to someone else's house, especially since she was just a young woman. So my mom went to the room my dad was sleeping in to tell him someone was knocking on the door. He woke up shocked, as if something grave had just happened. His eyes bulged, bloodshot red, and he thought, *Maybe it's the police.* He went to the front door to see who it was. Then in relief, he opened the door and saw that it was just Sha. He felt the weight of the world fall off his shoulders.

When Sha came inside, my dad wanted to talk to him. "I need a burka," said my dad.

"What do you need a burka for?" Sha asked.

"I need to help my cousin run away so we can get married together," my dad replied. My dad and his cousin had a very deep love for each other.

"Forget her, friend. I'll find you a beautiful girl so you can marry her here," said Sha to my dad.

"Will she even accept?" asked my dad.

"Of course she will accept. I will talk to her for you," said Sha. After Sha finished the conversation with my dad, He went to my grandma every day, telling her, "Sister, please arrange a marriage between your daughter and my friend." Sha asked for one week straight.

My grandma replied, "No, I can't. I don't know who he is and who he isn't. I don't know what kind of person he is."

Sha said, "I promise my friend is a really good guy." Sha was really upset at my grandma. He then went to his room to talk to my dad to give him the news. "She's not accepting your marriage proposal."

When my dad heard they didn't want to go through with the marriage, he took the matter in his own hands. He sent a bunch of goons with guns to Sha's house, where my grandma was staying. "If anyone says anything about declining the marriage proposal, I will shoot and kill everyone in this house!" the goons exclaimed. My mom's grandpa saw the goons go into the house while he was on the way to Sha's house, so he started rushing to his house.

"Son, you don't ask for a marriage while holding your guns and threatening someone's life. Go bring your mother and father," said my mom's grandpa to my dad and his goons. My dad noticed sending the goons actually worked in his interest. My dad then heard my mom's grandpa out. He ended up leaving, along with his goons.

The next day came around, and my dad brought his parents to my mom's grandpa's house for the marriage proposal. They started talking about how they would move past this situation, eventually leading to agreeing to the proposal. The marriage was expected to occur twenty-five days later. A lot of the members of my grandma's family did not approve of this marriage. Even my mom's grandpa went to Sha's house, which was a couple-minute walk, to talk to my dad.

Every day until then, my mom argued with my grandma, "I don't want to marry anyone! I'm only seventeen years old! Please don't make me go through with this."

My grandma didn't say a word to Fiaza and simply forced Fiaza to get married to a person who had killed a man. One day, the man who was soon to become my dad came to sit down with my grandma while my mom was with her. My dad just talked to my grandma.

"Go get some chai for us," said my grandma to Fiaza.

"I don't want to make it," said my mom.

My dad noticed my mom being disobedient. "She's arguing a lot. I hope she won't start big arguments with me back at my home," said my dad to my grandma.

"No, no, she's a really good girl. She will take care of

you. Whatever you want her to do, she won't say a word. She will get the job done," my grandma replied. My dad got the reassurance he needed and was happy. He then left to go back to his house.

The reason my mom was arguing with my grandma was because she loved someone else. Fiaza could not tell her mom she loved someone else. She was gravely ashamed of herself. *How can I tell her?* Fiaza thought.

Eventually, twenty-five days later, it was time for my mom to marry my dad. While they were at the ceremony, Fiaza's sister Zenath came with her husband and his family. Zenath's husband's family destroyed the decorations around the ceremony because they didn't want Fiaza to get married.

"Hey! There is a marriage going on in this house. Please don't do this. You're ruining a marriage," said my grandma. However, they wanted Fiaza to marry their son. Fiaza looked up and saw all the commotion. She noticed none of her family members were there besides her grandparents and her mom, because no one else approved of the marriage. They finally got married. Due to my dad being wanted in Sialkot, he and his newlywed wife were forced to relocate to Gujranwala along with his family. The day after they officially moved there, Fiaza's mom and her two little sisters, Sadia and Shazia, came to visit my mom. They brought a feast of food, which was part of their tradition when someone got married.

One of my mom's little sisters used to share the same bed with her, which is why she wanted to go with my grandma, so she could spend the night with my mom. Shazia was begging my mom to let her stay there with her for a while, because she missed the bond they had together. My mom then asked my dad's older sister Khalda if Shazia could stay with them for a little bit.

"No, it's not in our tradition to have your sister live with us," said Khalda. My mother got really depressed. While she was doing chores around the house, Khalda told my mom to go grab her some water. My mom went to get the water, and due to her being in her feelings, she accidentally dropped and broke the jug of water. "Stand up straight and work properly, or else I'll handle you," said Khalda. With tears rolling down her eyes, Fiaza ran to her mom to tell her what Khalda said about her sister not being able to stay with them because of their tradition. My grandma understood the situation, so she ended up leaving with her two daughters, leaving my mom there with my dad's family.

The next day, my dad and Fiaza went to her parents' house with my dad's family. They all had a feast together. Even though my grandma didn't have much money, she went out of her way to buy clothes for Fiaza, my dad, and his whole family. Then they all went back home to Gujranwala.

"Your grandpa makes a lot of furniture. You should've brought some of that furniture to our house," said Amra, one of my dad's sisters. She was expecting much more than Fiaza's family had to offer, because my grandma had four daughters and one son. Her son was the only one she and her whole family could depend on for getting money to keep the household together. One day, Amra asked my mom to open up her suitcase so she could see what she had. My mom opened up her suitcase. The clothes she had gotten from my dad's side of the family were out of style, used, and dirty. My dad's sisters saw the clothes and started going through them, each one claiming a dress was theirs. "Whoever's clothes these are, you can have them," said my mom to my dad's sisters. Every time Fiaza sat near them, they made fun of her appearance.

Amra told my mom to ask my dad to send us a TV because we didn't have one. My mom called and told her husband, "We need a TV here. Can you send one for us?" A week later, they received the TV.

When my dad's other sister Khalda found out, she started a huge argument with my mom. "Who is he? Who listens to his wife more than his sister?" said Khalda. She kept spouting disgusting comments about my dad. Khalda then took the TV so no one else could use it. After she used the TV for some time, the TV burned out and stopped working. My mom didn't have a say in it. She could only listen and go back to her room and harm herself. They treated my mom like a maid. They loafed around and had my mom do all the chores around the house. As time went on, my father's older sister forced my mom to do all the chores around her house, such as cleaning stairs that were filthy and washing her clothes until three in the morning. She would wake my mom up at the crack of dawn and force her to cook and clean at both houses.

This was around the time my mom was pregnant with me. It was also around the time they found out my mom wasn't a virgin. Knowing that, they mistreated her even more. She loved someone other than my dad, and her whole world had flipped upside down. Her dreams of marrying the one she loved were shattered before her eyes. She hated the fact that she was forced to marry my dad. She couldn't voice what she was thinking because she would just bring about unnecessary consequences.

Nine months later, my mom gave birth to me at the hospital, on May 2, 1988. When she went home the next day, I fell off the bed when my mom fell asleep due to her not getting any sleep prior to my birth. I started crying, which caused Dad's older sister to come in and take me every day after that. She would only let my mom see me when I was hungry, and then she would take me back after my mom fed me.

5

A CHILD IS BORN (ME)

FROM THE TIME OF MY birth, I was an ill child. A series of breathing issues followed me into this world, and at one point, I had continuous diarrhea and a constant fever of 105 degrees. Khalda took my mom and me to a college that she was teaching at in Pallandri, Pakistan, which was fifteen hours away, when I was not feeling well. We all stayed there for a year and a half. At that time, my mom and Khalda gave me medicine here and there. My fever was on and off. While my mom and Khalda were in Pallandri, I got really sick again. Khalda and my mom took me to Wah Cantt to Khalda's aunt's house. They spent a night there.

The day after, Khalda and my mom took me to a renowned doctor in a town called Rawalpindi that was near Wah Cantt. He ran tests and took some blood. When the result came in, he could not find what was making me so sick. Khalda then took my mom and me back to her aunt's house in Wah Cantt. Khalda went to Pallandri by herself, leaving my mom and me with her aunt, in hopes of me getting rest and getting better. After five to six days, Khalda came back to pick us up and took us back to Pallandri. Khalda would go to the college, and after she was done teaching, she would come back with her friend Zada. After Khalda would hang out with Zada for a couple of hours, Khalda would always have my mom cook food for them while they talked and had a good time. Then after they were done, Khalda had Fiaza walk her friend back to the college thirty minutes away, where she stayed in a hostel. Then she would walk all the way back during sunset. After two days of walking back and forth with Khalda's friend, my mom said to Zada, "I'm taking you home, but who's going to walk back with me?" Zada didn't say anything and went into her hostel.

My mom did this for at least three weeks after that. Around that time, my dad came to visit his family in Gujranwala. He noticed my mom and Khalda weren't there, but he wanted to see me because I was so sick. One of his family members told him where we went, and then he made his way to Pallandri. My dad got to Khalda's house, and they were talking. Zada was also there. "Why don't you get married to my brother?" said Khalda to Zada, because Zada was educated and my mom had no education. Khalda then noticed it was dusk, so she asked Fiaza to take Zada home. Fiaza went and then came back.

After two to three days, my mom and dad took me back to Gujranwala. About a week later, my grandpa from my dad's side invited a family with a few sons to dinner and talked about arranging a marriage for his daughter Amra. The family's dad really liked Amra. "I want to arrange a marriage for my son to your daughter," said the family's dad.

Once they ate, the family went back home. Then the next day, my dad's family went over to that family's house to meet the son and see how everyone was as a family. They all had a small feast and then went home. After staying in Gujranwala for two months, my dad went back to Saudi Arabia for work. A month went by, and Amra got married. Then Amra went back home to her newlywed husband's house.

Not long after, my mom noticed she was pregnant again. When my grandma found out, she came to visit every other week with Shazia to make sure she was doing OK. Shazia wanted to see the video of Amra's marriage. "Can I see the video of the marriage please?" Shazia asked my mom.

My mom went to ask Rafea, my dad's other little sister. "Rafea, my sister wants to watch the video of Amra getting married. Can we watch it?" my mom asked.

"There's a lock on the TV stand door. And I think Khalda has the keys," Rafea replied.

My mom just stayed quiet and went back to Shazia and my grandma in the other room. "Rafea said the key to the VCR is with Khalda, so we can't watch it right now."

"Damn! I wanted to see what I looked like while dancing!" said Shazia.

Then my mom went shopping at the bazaar with Shazia and their mom. After two hours of shopping, they all came home. My grandma, my mom, and Shazia saw Rafea showing the video of the marriage to her friend. My mom was furious. *When I asked if I could show my sister the video, she wanted to act like she didn't have the key. But when her friend wanted to watch the video, she had the key,* my mom thought. Whenever my grandma came over, no one in my dad's family came out to see my grandma. They would see my grandma and not even say hi to her. My dad's mom would sit with Fiaza's mom for just five to ten minutes and then go back to doing whatever she was doing. None of them wanted my mom's family to come over. My grandma and Shazia ended up going back home because they didn't feel welcomed. They wouldn't let my mom go see them either.

While my mom was pregnant with my other brother, it was a constant working routine: cooking and cleaning the floor, the bathroom, and everyone else's clothes. Khalda told my mom that the more she worked, the easier it would be to deliver the baby. Khalda would then convince her younger brother to tell my mom to do more work around the house. He would get my mom to make chicken. Once the chicken was made, my mom would sit down for less than an hour, and he would ask her if she could make him roti. Then she would go get the flour ready so she could make it. After she washed her hands and got ready to sit down, he would come back again. "Can you wash my pants?" Then my mom had to hand-wash the clothes. As soon as my mom was almost done washing the pants, he would come back with a shirt. "Can you wash this too please?" She would wash the shirt, and he would come back a fourth time asking her to iron the clothes she had just washed. While they were soaking wet. After she ironed the clothes she had washed for a whole hour, he would come back with socks that needed to be washed. "Can you wash and iron these too?" He did this on and off for a week.

One day, Amra came to my mom at ten o'clock at night, asking if she could sew up a dress for her. She stayed up all night sewing it for Amra. It took my mom three whole hours to finish. When Amra woke up in the morning, she took the suit and went to school to teach. A day went by, and my mom caught me constantly wetting my hair under the sink and styling it. She got mad because she knew I was prone to getting sick. She grabbed me by the arm and took me outside to bathe me. I started crying, and Amra noticed

"Why are you being such a smartass all of a sudden?" Amra said.

"Yeah, so what? I am a smartass," my mom replied. A few hours went by, and my mom noticed Amra hadn't said a single word to her. My mom then went to Amra and apologized for what she said.

"You have just been very sharp tongued lately," Amra replied.

My mom got quiet and went back to her room. About nine months later, when I was about two years old, on August 30, 1990, my brother was born. I got very sick again after he was born. My dad's older sister Khalda took me to every doctor in Pakistan over the span of three years so they could try to diagnose the problem. All of the doctors Khalda went to had no idea what was going on. However, the last doctor they went to knew exactly who could help.

He recommended an American doctor, Dr. Sonia, who had her own infirmary in Pakistan. Khalda took me to see her, about thirty minutes away. Dr. Sonia was able to see me immediately. She ran tests and did some bloodwork and then sent us home while she waited on the results. Two days later, Dr. Sonia gave Khalda a call. "The test results are ready. You can come by, and bring the child." Khalda went back to Dr. Sonia to see what the problem was. She told Khalda that my liver was a few inches bigger than normal and that I had aplastic anemia. I wasn't producing enough red blood cells. "Keep him away from filthy and dusty areas," Dr. Sonia recommended. She prescribed medicine to hold me over and gave it to Khalda. She told Khalda that I wouldn't survive long if I stayed in Pakistan, because the medical industry wasn't advanced enough to find the underlying causes of my breathing issues. I needed to get to America or the United Kingdom for treatment. When

Khalda got home, she called my dad and broke the news to him. My dad said he was going figure something out, and that became his main purpose.

My mom saw that Khalda was on the phone, so she seized the opportunity to sneakily ask her father-in-law if he could call her mom and get her to come visit her. "You saw her two weeks ago, and you're already sad?" asked my mom's father-in-law jokingly.

"Yes, I miss her really badly. Can you call her?" asked my mom.

My mom's father-in-law then called my grandma for my mom while he was at work because he didn't want Khalda finding out. Khalda never allowed my mom to be in contact with her family since her marriage. Because she had my mom doing all the chores around the house, if she left, there would be no one to do the chores around both houses. My mom's father-in-law agreed because he knew what Khalda was doing was wrong.

My grandma ended up visiting my mom around eleven or twelve o'clock in the afternoon. She got my mom some clothes, too, before my mom had to start her daily chores. My mom's brother Javed came with my grandma because he was living in Kuwait. It was his first time meeting my mom's kids. Javed brought a bunch of presents for her kids, lots of clothes. When Fiaza saw her mom, she was overjoyed and vented to her about how her husband's relatives were treating her, to which she replied, "Have some hope, and put your trust in God. It'll get better someday."

When my father's relatives noticed my grandma arriving at their house, they didn't speak with or welcome her, showing no hospitality. They just had cooked potatoes sitting on the counter, with nothing else with it. My dad's relatives would usually cook a feast containing all different kinds of meat for their friends and family that came over. But when my grandma came over, they didn't even think about cooking food for her, so my mom would have to give her leftovers from the night before. Once my grandma and Javed left that day, my mom got sad and just went to her room because she couldn't go back over there. My dad's sisters would take all of my mom's brand-new clothes that had been given to her by my grandma, wear them, and give them back used and worn.

A month went by of Fiaza missing her mom before she asked her father-in-law to take her to see her mom again. He suggested asking Khalda first because she was hotheaded. My mom asked him, "Who is older, you or her?" So he decided to take Fiaza to her mom's house without consulting Khalda. It was about an hour away. As soon as they got there, my dad's sister Rafea called her dad, saying Khalda was livid.

"Why didn't you get permission to leave?" Khalda asked. So my mom visited her mom only for a short time because they were rushing them to go back. When they got back, Khalda started yelling at both my mom and her dad. "What if I took her? There's no problem!" said my mom's father-in-law. My mom apologized out of fear and said she'd never make the same mistake again. After that incident, she was back to her old routine, constantly doing work around the house.

Shortly after my dad arrived in Gujranwala, Pakistan, from Saudi Arabia because he obtained a visa to get to the United States, my grandma came to visit him. "Why don't you find me another girl to marry?" said my dad jokingly to my grandma.

My grandma replied, "Why should I find you another girl? Go ask your sisters to find one for you."

"Why should we do it? You go do it yourself," said Amra, with a disgusted look on her face. Arma then got up and walked away enraged, making a big deal out of the whole situation.

My dad ran after Amra. "Who is she to say something like that to us?"

My dad came back after talking to his sister. "Come on, let's go. You have to apologize for what you said," he told my grandma. Then she went to the room where Amra and her other sisters were and apologized for saying the things she said. My grandma left after she apologized because she felt that she had been disrespected, knowing she didn't do anything wrong.

During this time, my dad was heavily associated with crime, murder, and his gang. He ended up being on the top of Pakistan's wanted list, dead or alive. Somehow he was able to leave the country and flee to Saudi Arabia.

Shortly after, my dad left to go to the United States alone, leaving my mom, my younger brother, and me behind at my dad's family's house. She was stuck with the same work routine for three and a half, almost four years. During this time, my mom was still not allowed to see any of her relatives.

"Can you please call my mom? I want her to come here because I miss her," she said to her father-in-law.

"OK, sure, I'll call her." While my dad was in the United States, Fiaza had her mom come visit her every two weeks because she was lonely and didn't have anyone there with her.

One day, my mom's father-in-law came into her room to wake her up. "Let's go. Get ready so I can take you to meet your mom." My mom quickly got up and got ready to go over to Sialkot to meet her.

When my mom got there, no one was home. "Maybe they're at my mom's sister's house?" said my mom to her father-in-law.

On the way there, they stopped halfway to the destination and saw a lady in a rickshaw. "Everyone got together and went to Akbarabad because I think their mom passed away," said the lady on the rickshaw to my mom and her father-in-law.

My father-in-law knew my mom's grandma had passed away. "Yeah, I think someone did pass away," said Fiaza's father-in-law. Instead of going to my grandma's sister's house, they went straight to Akbarabad. When my mom got there, she looked ahead and saw her grandma lying there, dead, with everyone sitting around her sobbing. My mom just stood there in disbelief. She started crying, feeling the pain of losing the one she was closest to. Not even letting my mom stay with her family, my mom's father-in-law said, "Let's go back home." It was around four or five that evening when my mom got back home to Gujranwala with my dad's relatives.

When my mom got home, she noticed me in the hallway, arms crossed and crying. "My grandma is gone! My grandma is gone!" I cried repeatedly.

Four months later, my dad called Khalda. "I'm gonna send my wife and my son Mannie a couple of passports. There's a family coming from America, and they're letting me use their passport so you can come with them. They'll be there in a couple days."

In America, he had started working for a taxi company to make a living and save money. Through this taxi career, he had become close with several families. He convinced one of the families to allow him to use their wife's and son's passports by telling them about my health situation. "My son is having breathing issues, and he won't make it unless I can get him to the States and figure out what's causing the issues."

One week later, the family that was coming gave my dad's side of the family a call after they got settled in, letting them know when to be ready to be picked up. "We're going to come in less than a week, so be ready to leave," said the family.

My mom's father-in-law came down to tell her the good news. "Let's go. Get ready so you can see your mom. I don't

know when you'll be able to see her again, so let's go now."
Once Fiaza arrived at her mom's house, she stayed there for a
little over an hour. They ate food together for the last time.
"It's almost time. We should really get going. You still have to
pack all your stuff," said my mom's father-in-law. My grandma
got really sad and started crying because her daughter had to
leave. My mom got on her father-in-law's motorcycle to leave.
My grandma followed her out, and as they were leaving, my
grandma stayed there until Fiaza was out of sight.

A couple of days later, the family that came with my and my
mom's passport showed up at my dad's family's house. There
were only two passports they could use, one from the wife
and one from a young son. My dad told my mom that she had
to come with their oldest son, me, because I was the one with
health complications. My brother would have to wait to go to
the United States. My mom didn't want to leave him behind,
even though she didn't have a choice. My dad promised her
that he would get my brother into the country after we got
there first.

My mom was forced to leave my younger brother behind.
They picked my mom and me up and took us to Karachi. She
stayed in Karachi for one month with the family's grandma.

"Your son doesn't really match the photo on the passport.
What if he can't get on the plane? What will you do then?"
asked the family's grandpa.

"If he doesn't go, then I won't go either," my mom replied. Everyone stayed quiet. At the end of the month, my mom was getting ready to board the plane. Thankfully, my mom and I made it through without a problem and were able to get on the plane. In 1994, we arrived at the airport in New York. Airport security separated us all so they could check everyone's passports and then eventually let us through. When my mom and I got out of the airport, I saw my dad standing there waiting for us.

6

THE AMERICAN DREAM

WE ARRIVED AT THE HOUSE of the family that helped me and my mom get to America. We spent the night there before heading off. The next day, my dad got us and his friend Krish and drove us all the way to his house in Virginia. We then arrived at his apartment, stayed there for a month and a half, and stayed there for about two months with Krish. Krish wanted his wife to come over to my dad's house in Virginia. He called her, talked to her for a bit, and then eventually arrived at my dad's apartment in Virginia. Life was going well, and my mom and I were getting by happily.

Around this time, my mom started to feel really bad for leaving my younger brother. She still couldn't believe she had to leave him. Krish's kids and I would play a lot in the mornings, and then my dad would get really mad because he didn't get sleep. "Stop making noise! I'm trying to sleep!" he'd yell. The reason my dad was upset was because he would sleep during the day and then drive a taxi all night. Arya told them to shut up because he was asleep.

Then my dad got my mom pregnant again. Every time there was work around the house, Krish's wife would not let my mom do any of it. My dad eventually told us we had to leave this house because the rent was too high. He started applying in a neighborhood that was an hour away from his apartment to rent a house for his family. About five to six months later, they were able to approve my dad for the house.

My dad started taking me to the doctors to figure out what was causing the breathing issues. They ran CAT scans, did physicals, and more but couldn't tell what was behind my medical issues. They simply told my parents it was asthma. A few months after my mom and I arrived, my dad was able to get my brother into the US the same way.

We lived in the ghetto of Alexandria, Virginia, when we first got here. My dad registered us for a school called Mount Vernon Woods, and I remember starting school as a second grader. My brother started in kindergarten. We didn't really have anything to wear when we first moved here, so my dad took me and my brother to Walmart for some clothes and shoes. In the beginning, I had a hard time understanding English, so I also attended ESOL (English speakers of other languages) classes. These were classes for kids who had English as their second language.

The kids in school bullied me. Every day, I got picked on because I couldn't speak English and because the clothes and shoes I had on weren't name brands. The kids would make comments like, "Oh, you have on Route 66 Walmart jeans," to insult me. Getting bullied was a daily occurrence, and I would come home crying and pleading with my mom to make it stop. My dad's English wasn't good either, but my mom had him call the school, informing them of the situation. Nevertheless, the bullying persisted, and I had to learn to endure it.

One day, my brother and I were watching TV when suddenly we heard our mom scream. We ran into the room to find that my dad was slapping her in the face. He yelled and told us, "Stay the fuck on the couch," as he dragged my mom by the hair into their room. We heard our mom screaming as she was being beaten half to death. All we could do was cry helplessly as we sat on the couch, not daring to disobey our dad. That was our first time witnessing domestic abuse. Little did we know that it soon would become a daily occurrence, leaving us conditioned to this harsh reality.

My English slowly got better, but the bullying never stopped. I got on the patrol squad and gave morning announcements in school. I still remember getting outstanding awards for passing all my classes with straight As. In the fourth grade, the other kids bullied me so much that I broke down crying in class. The teacher often stood up for me, telling the other kids to stop bullying me.

One day, my dad's brother from Pakistan called him. He handed my brother the phone because he wanted to talk to him while my dad was asleep. When my brother was on the phone, I vaguely remember throwing something at him as a joke. He quickly started crying, which woke up my dad. The next thing I knew, my dad yelled, "Get the fuck over here." As I walked to him, I trembled in fear. I was thrown on the bed as his hand reached out, grasping my neck. Then I felt his spare hand, hard and cold, beating down on my face. I felt my face turn blue as I gasped for air. Then I got pushed off the bed and was kicked through the hallway until I ended up in the living room. He threw me on the couch and then grabbed the broomstick and started hitting my legs until the stick broke. I fell to the ground, crying helplessly.

A couple of months later, my dad opened up a buffet-style restaurant somewhere in DC. He hired a cook to work and clean around the kitchen. About eight months passed, and everything was going great until a few guys came to hang out at his restaurant. My dad thought they would grab some plates and get some food for themselves. But he thought wrong. As my dad was putting food into the trays, he looked out from the kitchen and saw a bunch of alcohol bottles. The guys were simply hanging out in the dining area, drinking alcohol, which was not allowed under any circumstance. My dad came out and told them, "I don't know what you guys think you're doing, coming in here thinking you can drink at my restaurant. You all have to go someplace else."

"Nah, we're gonna drink here," the drunks replied.

"No, you have to get the fuck out of my restaurant," my dad replied. The drunks got really angry and started flipping tables and throwing chairs and anything else they could get their hands on. Then My dad grabbed a 2x4 and started beating the drunks with it until they ran away.

My dad pressured my mom to act as the cook so he wouldn't have to hire a cook.

The abuse never stopped. Eventually, I remember moving to a small town called Woodridge in Virginia. I started school and was still in the process of learning English. The kids continued to bully me, and in the meantime, I had an abusive dad to deal with, which only made things worse. Although I had become good friends with a neighbor, my dad limited our freedom and rarely allowed us just to be kids and go outside. One day, I was walking home from where the bus had dropped me off. I saw Caleb on the way there. He wanted me to stay outside and play, but I couldn't, so I told him I had to be back home before my dad got there. "My dad doesn't let me play outside," I said to Caleb. Caleb was curious as to why, so I told him everything about my dad being abusive and excessively violent toward my family and me. I had Caleb come over to my house for safety reasons, hoping my dad wouldn't beat me if he saw my friend was there.

We were still incredibly poor and never seemed to have a set of clean clothes. I vaguely remember waking up and having to get the roaches out of my shoes. My peers would often make comments about what I was wearing, and I eventually learned how to tune those comments out.

Around this time, my dad started a wholesale business where he would sell gas stations certain necessary supplies. He forced me to go on these trips with him even though the last thing I wanted to do was be around my abusive father. One day, I missed my bus ride home, so I took a route through the woods to get home as quickly as possible. As I was walking, I noticed a few bullies from school. I couldn't go around them, so they started to kick me and push me around. I remember stepping through the front door, dirt and grime from the woods covering me. As soon as I saw my dad's face, I knew that another beating was inevitable. At this point, my life was a never-ending nightmare that I couldn't seem to escape.

One day, my dad brought home this lady I had never met before. My mom questioned my dad about the woman, but he dodged her questions. My mom got the lady's number, as she was supposed to take my sister and brother out. Then my mom asked me to call the lady to question the relationship between her and my dad. I did as my mom asked and gave the woman a call.

Right after we got off the phone, the woman called my dad to let him know about me calling and asking her questions about their relationship. That day, my dad came home and screamed my name, telling me to come to him. I was scared and wasn't sure why. As he started beating me, he started asking me why I called her and tried to pull information out of her. He told me never to call her again.

At this point, I began skipping school as some sort of escape from my home life. One day, the school called my dad and told him I wasn't in class. My dad spotted me on the street near my school. He told me to get in the car and started hitting me and yelling at me. After the repeated beatings and verbal abuse, I started feeling numb. Due to my absence from school, the district sent a social services person to question me. I admitted that my troubling home life was the reason behind my poor performance in school. The next day, social services and a police officer showed up at my front doorstep while my dad was at work. My mom opened the door and phoned my dad, saying social services was there and wanted to talk to him. He threatened my mom to keep quiet or else he would harm her and kill her family back home. She knew he was capable of doing that, so she kept quiet and denied everything. When I heard my mom denying everything, my heart broke. I realized I had become the sacrifice so my mom's family wouldn't get killed.

My dad told my mom to call him after they left so he could speak to me. I was so afraid that I was planning to run away from the house before my dad came home because I knew it was going to be a nightmare. When my mom found out I was packing to leave, she convinced me to stay, out of fear of my dad. My mom called my dad after the social services people left, and he told her to hand me the phone. I was petrified. He started cussing me out, saying, "You think I give a fuck about the cops? Ima beat the fuck out of you when I get home." After he hung up, the time started racing as I waited for him to walk through the door.

When my dad came home that evening, he said to Caleb, "You can go home." He was yelling at me and my mom in Urdu. Caleb didn't understand what he was saying, and he acted like he was leaving and shut the front door but stayed inside to see what would happen. He went back to the living room where my dad was hitting me on the head with a hard plastic phone and a rubber shoe, but he didn't know exactly why or what he was yelling in Urdu. When Caleb saw my dad hitting me on the head, he realized the things I had been telling him were all true.

My father was physically abusive and violent. We were stuck in a vicious cycle and lived in a constant state of fear. When my dad saw Caleb was still there, he said to him, "I told you, you can go home." Caleb then pleaded for my dad to hit him instead, trying to get my dad to stop hitting me. I convinced Caleb to leave, telling him that I was used to it. Caleb eventually left, and my dad continued to beat me to the point of unconsciousness.

Caleb went home and told his parents what was happening, and Caleb's parents came over to my house to talk to my parents.

Then one of Caleb's brothers called the cops. When the police came, once again my mom got scared of my dad and told the police there was no abuse going on. The cops ended up leaving. Later, I told Caleb if my mom ever told the police about what was happening, my dad would have his gang members back in Pakistan kill my mom's family. Then Caleb started to see how bad my situation actually was. It seemed as if everyone was powerless to help me and my family. The next day at school, the cop wanted to talk to me, so they called me into the security office. He assumed I was lying about my dad abusing me, because of my attendance record. "You could get in trouble for lying to the law like that," the cop said. So I made up excuses to explain the head wounds. At that point, I started feeling helpless.

I remember one day after school, my brother had gotten a failing grade in one of his classes. The news had reached my dad from a family friend who had translated the call that came from our school. That day when we got home, my dad started beating my brother. I grabbed his hand in desperation, to stop him from continuing. Instead of stopping, he redirected the focus of his heavy hand from my brother to me and continued to beat me, asking me why I had grabbed his hand. Every day, it felt like a never-ending cycle. We lived in fear twenty-four seven but were sometimes able to muster up some hope that better days were to come.

7

IN TROUBLE WITH THE LAW

EVENTUALLY, MY DAD WANTED TO move to another district. I ended up repeating the ninth grade twice because I skipped a lot of school.

We eventually moved to the city, Fredericksburg in Virginia, where my dad opened a tobacco shop and forced me and my brother to work. There were certain customers from New York who would purchase large quantities of cigarettes. We were tasked with drafting up the invoices, and we began charging the customers on top of their orders so we could save up some money. We started putting the money toward better clothes and shoes. Slowly, our social status at school started changing.

One day, a customer walked in with a blunt in his hand while my brother and I were managing the shop. We asked him what he was smoking, but he just dismissed us casually.

He asked for a hand pipe, and we asked him to trade us for some marijuana. He agreed. We got his contact information and started selling marijuana at the shop and making decent profits. One day, the guy pulled out a gun on us and told us if we ever snitched on him, he would come after us. We took it as a warning, but the money from selling marijuana was too good. Now going to the shop was worth it because we finally had our own income flowing. Regardless, our dad would force us to continue working for him.

In the tenth grade, I passed driver's ed and got my pink slip for the DMV to test for my learner's permit. When I got there, the DMV started questioning me about my social security number or birth certificate. I quickly realized I didn't have any of that on hand because I was an undocumented American. My other three siblings were born in the United States and already had birth certificates, and my father had already obtained his work permit. Until this point, I had never really understood my immigration status. My whole life had been centered around going to school without any other freedoms. I was never really allowed to have friends and never got to experience a typical American childhood. Due to my unfortunate childhood, all my willfulness was centered around making money, which molded me into the go-getter I am today.

We started selling marijuana to everyone we knew, and everyone on the block knew we had the best product. A couple of times, I fronted products to people because of the mutual trust we had established. When people started breaking that trust, I told them I wouldn't see them again. I started to realize that you can't form friendships with customers, as they would take advantage of that relationship. I got close to a couple of customers whom I deemed as good friends.

One of the guys called me to purchase an ounce. I told him to come by and to let me know when he got there. When he got there, I walked out with the ounce and got in his car. He started driving around, and suddenly, he said his car was messed up, so he pulled over. Immediately, a car pulled up behind us, and next thing I knew, someone had a gun to my head. They threatened me for the ounce, so I handed it over. He placed the product in his car and came back asking the other guy for his chain. They wanted to claim that it was a robbery, but this was a critical mistake because he went back to his car and came back. From the tone of the "robber's" voice, I could tell that they were in on it together.

There was another instance when I wanted to purchase a quarter pound from a guy I was close to. He was a frequent customer at the store, and we shared meals all the time. I asked him if he had any connections for marijuana. He said it would be $1,200 for a quarter pound, and the next day, he, his brother, and his friend pulled up to my dad's shop and told me to head out. I exchanged the cash for a backpack that I assumed carried the product inside. When I got home to check the weed, I saw that it was Styrofoam with grass wrapped around it. I couldn't believe someone I trusted had betrayed me, once again. I was able to get them back when I spotted their car in a neighborhood one day. A friend and I scratched up the car and flattened the tires to get even.

One day, my supplier was unavailable, and I had to outsource the product from someone I didn't know too well. He asked me for the money up front and told me he would bring the product after the money was in hand. Once I gave him the money, he never came back, and I quickly realized I had been scammed.

My mom started to figure out my little side business. When she confronted me, I told her I didn't have any choice. One day, I forgot there was a gram of weed on my dresser. When my mom was cleaning, she saw it and told me to put it away quickly before my dad saw it. I stashed it in my pocket and had to use the bathroom. When my dad came home, he asked my mom where I was, and she told him I was in the bathroom. He came downstairs to search my bedroom for money, and then after he couldn't find anything, he waltzed right into the bathroom I was in. He had set rules that we were not allowed to lock our doors.

While I was still seated on the toilet, he started questioning me, assuming I had stolen the money from the cash register in the shop. Earlier that day, he had been unable to spot any of the smaller bills that were used for change from the customers paying with only big bills. He then asked me to empty out my pockets, and as I was emptying them, I completely forgot I had the weed in my pocket. When he saw the weed, he became furious. His eyes just lit up, and he began viciously beating me and asking me where I got the weed from. As he continued slapping me, he told me to hurry up and get out. He assumed the weed was from one of his workers at the shop. At the point of utter confusion, I conceded to my dad that my brother knew about this situation. He ended up receiving a beating as well. I felt absolutely horrible when my brother started crying. Then my dad came back to me and continued asking where I got the weed. The beating lasted all evening, with my dad only taking one break to catch his breath. Eventually, I was in so much pain that I just told him what he wanted to hear, which didn't stop the beating. The next couple of days, I wasn't allowed to go to school since my dad didn't want any more trouble from social services, due to my face being bruised and cut up.

There were so many times when I contemplated ending my life. Once I grabbed a knife and put it up to my stomach, but ultimately, I couldn't see it through. I placed the knife back into its spot. Slowly, I started forming the hope that one day the endless abuse would end. One thing that always kept me going was knowing that there were people out there who had it worse than me.

A few stores down from where my dad's tobacco shop was, a Subway restaurant got raided by the DEA. The Subway workers were running an underground operation of cocaine sales, a few of whom I knew personally. We would sometimes trade cigarettes for Subway sandwiches. I received a blocked call from one of the workers to be careful since the cops were watching us. One of them ended up snitching on me and my brother, and I had to act as if I had no idea what they were talking about. I responded, "I have no idea what you are talking about. I didn't do anything."

One day, my brother and I needed to restock our product. That day, the cops ended up raiding my dad's tobacco shop. They tore up the whole shop looking for drugs but were unsuccessful, which infuriated them. My dad ended up getting charged for child labor since my brother was a minor. My dad and I were at home, but we went to the shop after hearing about the raid from my brother in a frantic phone call. The cops asked my dad if they could search the house, which he agreed to. Ironically, on that day, my supplier was on his way to drop off more products. When he reached my street, he saw the cop lights from a couple of feet away and made a quick U-turn. The DEA didn't find anything at our house, but my father ended up getting locked up on counts of child labor. It was the happiest moment of our lives.

However, the possibility of the abuse ending was quickly shattered when our dad posted bail and was promptly released the next day. The shop was all over TV and the newspaper due to the DEA raid and the charges of having a minor working at a tobacco shop. Due to this, the landlord did not want to continue the lease with my dad. Our family lost our only source of income, and we got behind on our mortgage payments. I received the majority of the blame from my dad for our financial situation. He would even tell my siblings I was to blame for the entire situation. The bank took our family to court for foreclosure on my family home because we were unable to make payments. The judge ruled that we had ten days to move out of the house and vacate the premises. Our entire family was on edge. I was particularly stressed because I needed to graduate that year, as I was about to turn twenty-one, and it was my last chance to get my diploma before I got kicked out of the school district.

8

FREE AT LAST (ALMOST)

MY DAD WANTED TO TAKE us to Maryland to live in his friend's basement while he figured things out. I was afraid that I would be unable to graduate if I switched school districts again. It was one day before the court-ruled deadline for us to vacate, and I was in my class seeing all my classmates happy and worry-free. I wondered why my life had been so unfortunate so far. Tears started to form in my eyes as I walked out of class, and I didn't realize that my teacher had followed me. She told me to stop, and I turned around. I confessed to her what was going on, with the domestic abuse, me being an undocumented American, the house being foreclosed on, and our dad wanting to relocate to Maryland. I also told her I wasn't sure if I'd be able to graduate if I switched school districts again, so she offered to let me stay at her house until I graduated. However, according to school policies, students were not allowed to stay with their teachers. She told her best friend about the situation, and her friend ended up agreeing to let me stay with her. I asked if my brother could also stay with her, and she agreed to let us stay until we graduated.

Eventually, my mom and my other siblings left with my dad to Maryland after I convinced my dad to let us stay another three to four months until we graduated. The lady we were staying with, Robin, found out about our situation and hired an immigration attorney. I started to realize that life was slowly improving for my brother and me. My brother ended up becoming a ward of the state, where the state essentially takes custody under court order. This helped him obtain his green card. Robin became my brother's legal foster mom.

However, since I was about to turn twenty-one, there was nothing they could do for me. I was left in a place of confusion and disappointment, further solidifying my sense of how unfortunate I was. I started to hang out with my high school friends again, just to gain the sense of freedom that I never had. One day, I got a frantic call from my sister saying that domestic abuse was still happening, so I told my teacher, Ms. Niles, about the situation. She kindly offered to allow them to move in with her and went to go pick up my siblings and mom. Finally, they were safe, and I didn't have to worry about them anymore, but my undocumented status still worried me.

One day, we got together to have a family dinner with my brother, teacher, her best friend, and her mom. I finished my food, so I asked my friends to come pick me up. This upset Ms. Niles, Robin, and her mom. They thought I didn't appreciate them, and it left a sour taste in their mouth. Robin told me I needed to start working. I started helping one of my friends by babysitting her kids, and she would sometimes allow my friends to come over. After a while, she no longer needed a babysitter. At this point, Robin told me I needed to find another job within the week or she would kick me out. I knew I wouldn't be able to get another job because I wasn't documented. Instead, I just acted as if I was searching for jobs while spending time with my brother as much as I could before our time together was up. I was incredibly low and hurt, knowing for the first time ever I would have to separate from my brother.

When the week was up and Robin kicked me out, I walked off with my head down, tears streaming down my cheeks. I had no idea where I was going to go. Suddenly, I decided to head to New York, in search of new opportunities. I had some tobacco pipes with me, leftover from the shop, which I ended up selling to someone at the gas station. With one hundred bucks in my pocket, I called my friend Josue, who gave me a ride to DC. From there, I caught a ride to Chinatown for twenty bucks. I ran into one of my dad's old friends in Times Square. I pleaded with him to find me a job and not tell my dad that he had run into me. He ended up getting me a job in Manhattan at a deli. I worked the graveyard shift, 6:00 p.m. to 6:00 a.m., twelve hours a day, for a mere four dollars an hour. I got to work by catching the F train, which was an hour to and from work.

My mom called me up one day to go visit them, and I ended up quitting the job at the deli. I went to visit family but was once again homeless, with no sense of direction. I called up one of my dad's old friends to ask for a job. He agreed and got me a job at his brother's furniture store he was managing. Some days I would move furniture, and some days I would stand at the intersection holding up a sign. I made five hundred bucks a week, while living with my dad's friend's brother. When the holidays came around, he left for vacation. He told me I could stay with his brother and his family until he got back, and we could start back up where we left off. So I agreed. When I heard he had gotten back from vacation, I tried calling him. But he stopped answering. After a while of staying with his brother's family, I started to feel like I was intruding on their family and personal space. So one day, I just picked up and left.

My teacher ended up losing her job for helping certain students pass their tests, and this resulted in her house being foreclosed. Ms. Niles had to move in with her friend Robin, causing my mom and siblings to move back in with my dad. Once again, I started receiving calls from my sister about the beatings my dad would give her, my mom, and other siblings. At that point, I was already homeless, hopping from one friend's house to the other. Eventually, I decided to head back home to sacrifice myself for my siblings, as I was already conditioned to my dad's beatings. I didn't want them to become like me. It was back to the cycle of abuse.

My dad ended up opening an auto shop with his partner, and once again, he made me work there. I was essentially forced to learn how to work on cars. I was unwilling, and I didn't want to waste my time if I wasn't making any money. I started asking his partner if he could find me a job somewhere else so I could make some money and because I didn't want to learn how to work on cars. He told me he would see what he could do. One of my biggest pet peeves is wasting my time and not getting ahead financially.

One day, my dad didn't have money for groceries, so he asked his partner if he could get groceries for our family. My dad made me go with his partner to get the groceries, but I forgot to get milk. My dad was incredibly upset and ended up beating me. Even though I was already old enough to fight back, the trauma from fifteen years of abuse prohibited me from doing so. I still feared him greatly.

My dad's partner eventually found me a job at a gas station in Maryland. I started working eighty-four hours a week for eight dollars an hour. After the first week, I got a threatening call from my dad to hand over my first paycheck so he could pay the bills. He started leaving voice mails and messages threatening to kill and beat me. I was terrified and told him to come pick up the check. This continued. He would leave me messages while harassing me for my paychecks. I was so frustrated that I threw my phone at a wall, and it shattered to pieces. Come to find out, even though he was taking my paychecks, he was still nine months behind on payments and had his lawyer extend the court dates so my family could evade eviction.

Eventually, they got a final eviction letter, and my dad just disappeared, leaving my mom and siblings homeless. My brother got a hotel room for the night, and thankfully, I had some money saved up, so I found a house on Craigslist that didn't require a credit check. My mom and siblings became my responsibility. I invested the money I had saved up from my job into a side business, selling clothes and trying to make some more income. The gas station owner was not happy. He felt that I wasn't completely focused on that job, so he ended up firing me.

I had some money saved up for the next few months of rent in case I couldn't find a job on short notice. The owner of another gas station reached out to me, knowing I was a hard worker. I took the job, knowing I was responsible for taking care of my family. The owner offered me nine dollars an hour and a room in the house he had for his employees. At that time, six months of free rent was a good deal, so I agreed. They came to my house and picked me up.

On my first day of working, I went back to go to sleep and woke up to something crawling and biting me. Come to find out, it was bedbugs. I was unable to sleep, and at work, it was hard to function, and I always felt like something was crawling on me. I ended up going to the owner about the bedbugs, but he didn't do anything about it at first. Eventually, I started going back to the gas station to sleep on the table just to avoid the bedbugs. However, I was awakened every time someone came through the door, making it hard to get some rest.

My mom asked me to come visit, and I asked her to pray that I would make it. My brother had allowed me to use his car, an '01 Eclipse Convertible Spyder, so I made my way to see them. Due to extreme exhaustion, I took two 5-Hour Energy shots before making my way there. However, I ended up falling asleep behind the wheel and going 90 mph toward a bunch of trees. I woke up in an empty field with the car totaled. My nose was bleeding, and my head hurt, but I was blessed to make it out alive. The cop at the scene thought I was intoxicated but ended up letting me leave since I wasn't. I called my mom and told her I had gotten into an accident and the car was totaled. Due to this, I was unable to visit them.

I headed back to work and had enough money saved up to move out of the bedbug-infested house and into my own apartment in Maryland. The owner decided to switch me to another location, and I had to hitch rides with a coworker to and from work. After the owner found out that I had moved into my own apartment, he asked my coworker to stop giving me rides. I started walking three miles to and from work and eventually made some friends who sometimes gave me rides. At that time, my brother was working at a sports and health gym and became close friends with the 7-Eleven owner close by. He asked for a job for me, and the owner agreed. I ended up leaving the Maryland gas station job so I could be closer to home. I could no longer afford my mom's house bills since the new job did not pay as well. I started looking for new places on Craigslist and found a basement for my family and me to move into.

I worked at 7-Eleven under my mom's social security number, which my dad got for her using fake documentation years before. The owner of the 7-Eleven played the lottery a lot. One day he accused me of the register being short and took my paycheck. I argued that there was no way, due to my previous experience working registers with no issues, but he still ended up keeping my paycheck. This left me behind on finances. Luckily, one day while I was working, a friend from high school walked in and asked if I still sold marijuana or wanted to get back into it. I told him my situation and said that I would love to get back into it, but I didn't have the money to afford it. He told me I didn't have to pay the money up front; he would give me the marijuana first, and I could pay him after. I agreed to the opportunity because it was another source of income that I could bring in on top of still working at 7-Eleven.

The owner did not manage the store correctly and kept gambling, leaving the business in the negative. This resulted in the owner's brother taking the store back from him. His brother kept me as a worker, so I was able to save up some money between working there and hustling marijuana on the side. This helped me move myself and my family out of the basement and into an apartment. I continued to hustle marijuana on the side, since the salary from 7-Eleven was not enough to provide for me and my family.

Most of the time, I had to work double shifts, just so I could provide for my family. Sometimes even after working double shifts and hustling, I still didn't have enough money for all the bills. This caused me and my brother to bump heads, due to him always partying, not caring, and ending up with the wrong crowd, not wanting to work. He didn't realize how hard it was for me to try to maintain everything. Mutual people we knew would come in and laugh and crack jokes about how I had no life. All I did was work at 7-Eleven. I didn't go to parties or enjoy life. I didn't let any of that bother me because my main focus was to remain focused. I had responsibilities I hadn't signed up for that still had to be fulfilled one way or the other.

On top of that, one day the homie who was fronting me the marijuana couldn't do so anymore. The operation he was part of got shut down due to his source getting caught up with the law.

9

TAKING MATTERS INTO MY OWN HANDS

ONE DAY, AN OLD FRIEND of my dad's found my number and called me, begging me to give my dad another chance. He told me my dad wouldn't do the things he did to us before and that he had changed his ways. I told him I'd think about it and would let him know. Then one day the friend came to visit and brought our dad with him. My dad promised to change and be better, but he never did. He went right back to his old ways. It is like the saying goes: you can't teach an old dog new tricks.

In order to avoid our dad, my brother and I would sleep in the car at night on the street. My brother was enjoying my mom's cooking one day when my dad went up and slapped his ear because he saw his new piercing. His earring fell out, and the piercing got infected. After that, my brother pushed my dad and simply walked out of the house. At least my brother still had his foster mother when he needed an escape. The apartment complex we stayed at got a lot of attention from the cops, as a lot of tenants sold marijuana. When my dad left to visit someone, I moved out with my brother and siblings to one of my employer's rental houses. At this point, I wasn't bringing in enough money to pay for all of the bills; I could only manage some of the bills. This meant that at all times, something was getting cut off, whether it was electricity, water, or gas. We would sometimes have to take cold showers because the gas had been cut off.

The owner knew I sold marijuana and offered to go into business together. He said he would buy ten pounds for me to sell, and we could split the profits fifty-fifty. I remember calling one of my contacts, who said it would be $38K for ten pounds. I agreed to this because I believed it could bring in more income so I could provide for my family better. We gave my contact $38K, and he brought ten pounds of weed. The owner only gave the contact $400 for the drop-off, which made him mad, as it was a huge risk to transport so much product. This left a sour taste in his mouth. I sold each pound for $5,400, which meant I should've received $7K from the split, but the owner only gave me $2K and kept the other $12K. This wasn't the original agreement, but at this point I was just grateful for the extra money to help me pay for my family's bills. The owner wanted to do another transaction, so I contacted the guy once again. He came and picked up the $38K and never pulled through with the product. The owner was essentially robbed, and I was stuck in the middle of it. I offered to help him make the money back, but at that point I was just risking my life for nothing.

I found the owner another contact to purchase from in an attempt to help him make his money back on something that had been caused by his own greed. There was a girl in my neighborhood who sometimes bought weed from me. We started talking, but it didn't last because she was going to Virginia Commonwealth University for her master's in social services. Her uncles told her there was no point in dating a 7-Eleven worker with no future. Since she was going to university, there was no point in dating someone irrelevant to her future. She agreed. When she told me that, those words became planted in my head and gave me a sense of motivation I had never had before. I had been abused and neglected for the majority of my childhood, and that only fueled the fire.

One day when I was at work, someone from California stopped by the 7-Eleven. I said, "Aye, I heard California has the best weed. Could you get me some?" The guy agreed, saying he could get me one pound for $1,200. I was shocked since a pound could go for $3,800 in Virginia wholesale. I would have to send the guy the money, and he would just mail the product to me, which made me hesitant, as I really didn't have the money to spare at the moment. I asked one of my buddies to go in with me so I wouldn't have to risk the entire amount.

I called this guy, asking where to send the money, and I gave him my word that if he was legit, we would keep coming back. After receiving the money, the guy shipped the package. When it arrived, we ended up selling the pound for $5,400 by selling it in smaller quantities, turning a $4,200 profit.

After running into this guy, I drifted away from the 7-Eleven owner, as I realized I was risking my life for nothing, all while helping him get his money back for something he caused himself. I brought my brother into this business, and we ended up saving $60K. I asked my 7-Eleven coworker if I could get boxes shipped to his address, and for each package, I would pay him $500. He agreed, since it was easy income. One day, a buyer came to me looking to purchase, so I asked my friend how much he would sell a quarter pound for. He told me $1,200, which made me mad, since I was letting him buy a whole pound for $1,200 and didn't make a single penny from those transactions, while he tried to make $700 profit from me. I ended up cutting him off and told him to go find his own supplier in California. He wanted to use my coworker's address, and I told him he could, but he would need to pay $500 per package.

Unfortunately, I didn't know he was grabbing the package straight from the mailman before it was dropped off to avoid paying the fee. The mailman ended up getting suspicious, and that day, I had a five-pound drop-off scheduled. Although I had a bad feeling, as if something was holding me off, I still went. The intuition was so strong at one point it made me walk past the package and toward the undercover cop car. However, I did not have my contacts in, so I couldn't see anyone in the car and went back to grab the package. As I was walking away with the package, cars swooped in from all directions, and officers came out with guns drawn, yelling at me to "Drop the box." An officer told me to reach for my phone, so it seemed as if I was grabbing a weapon, so another officer tased me. The officers ended up remembering me from ten years before when they raided my dad's tobacco shop.

When my brother came home on the school bus, he was wondering what the commotion was all about until he realized I was the one in handcuffs. After the realization hit, he called my mom, who called my other brother. He ran to the house to grab the safe that had money in it before the cops got to the house. Before I got locked up, I applied for DACA through a lawyer due to the Dream Act. As I was in handcuffs, I told my sister to take my younger brother, who was returning home from school, by the playground so he wouldn't see me getting locked up.

When I was locked up, my closest brother had to step up to the plate of being the father figure. He eventually broke down crying when he came to the realization of my reality and how much he would have on his plate. I was also detained by ICE, as I was undocumented, and my work permit was still processing. It was finally approved, and my brother got me a good defense lawyer who fought hard on my case. The charges were dropped to a misdemeanor of possession under an ounce, and I served my time.

I had just been released when people started hitting me up again for products. However, I passed my customers on to my brother, as I knew the cops would be watching me fresh out of jail.

At this time, I began focusing on my smoke shop, which I had opened up before I was locked up. With the money I had saved up, I started focusing on getting the store up and running. August 30, 2013, was the store's grand opening, my brother's birthday, and the start of a new chapter in my life. Little did I know it was going to become one of the most prestigious functioning glass art galleries in the country. This chapter of my life would completely change the game for me. New opportunities, new goals, new plans, and new love.

I chose to open a glass shop / smoke shop because I was familiar with it. I knew how to run a store because of my father's tobacco shop back in the day. With the money I earned from hustling and working my ass off, I was able to open my store in Richmond, Virginia. The reason behind this location is funny, because my ex went to college there. In a way, I wanted to show her what she had lost after being heavily influenced by the ignorance of her family. What's better than making yourself feel better by showing someone, "Hey, look what you missed out on!"?

When you lose something, there's always something better out there for you. You just have to grab life by the horns and go for it. This is where my future ex-wife, Jayme, comes into the picture. At the grand opening of the shop, I met this girl through one of our mutual friends. She tells me till this day that the moment she met me, she knew we were going to end up together. I guess when you know, you know. She was actually interested in the guy she was at the shop with. We got to know each other through our mutual friends and started conversations through Facebook, Instagram, and so on. We really clicked and hit it off. She was a bartender at a local Richmond bar, and the more we got to know each other, the more we realized we wanted to try to have a relationship with each other. She was a really cool, down-to-earth chick, and we had a lot in common mentally, spiritually, and emotionally, as we both are Tauruses.

I realized I needed help at the shop and wanted to offer her a job to help me manage the store. I asked her to quit her job and come work for me. It wasn't anything like a knight-in-shining-armor kind of thing, just more of a great opportunity for me to get some support in what I envisioned for the shop. The other reason I offered her the job was because her managers just weren't treating her right. I have a big heart, and it hurt me to see her trying to bust her ass every day and not really be happy. So she ended up quitting her job and started working at the shop. She really saw the potential in me and the shop, and she had faith in it. She knew she could organize the shop better and pull her weight in the things I wasn't so good at. We made a good team and started building up the business.

I lived in Fredericksburg, Virginia, and the store was in Richmond, which was about an hour's drive every day. At the time, she was living in an apartment outside of the city but was soon moving downtown with her roommate. Around this time, I was looking to buy a puppy. I gave her a choice on which pup I should get. She helped me pick one out of the two that were available. This pup would be later known as the store's mascot, Boss. Since she was helping me at the shop, she had a little more free time to take care of a dog. She loved animals and was a huge dog person. She and I split time with Boss. On some weekends, I let her keep him with her, and she would come by and visit me at the shop. We would spend all day and almost all night at the shop. Boss was such a great worker too!

Since I lived an hour away, sometimes I would sleep at the shop. Eventually, when she moved downtown, I ended up moving in with her and her roommate so I could be closer to the store and run it the way I needed to.

Most smoke shops were using China-made glass for the tobacco pipes, and I wanted to innovate toward American-made glass. I took the advice of my consumers and started carrying products from a local artist who produced with American-made glass. As I started getting deeper into the industry, I realized the glass industry was bigger than I had originally expected. A local artist told me about a convention in Vegas called the Age Show, where artists across the globe went to sell their works to shop owners. Hearing that, I decided to sign up for the convention and make the trip to Vegas.

At the convention, Jayme and I began networking with different glass artists, learning about their products and promoting the smoke shop. This convention opened my eyes regarding this industry and helped me grow my business. When I realized how other shop owners were flipping art pieces, I knew I had to get in the game to really level up. There were certain artists whom the shop owners would crowd around, and that was an indication to me that those were the more popular artists I would need to network with so I could get the chance to carry their glass at my shop. At that point, the majority of the hot artists would not give me the time of day, knowing I didn't have much money to spare. They would often tell me to just hit them up on Instagram instead of giving me their phone number, which was an indication of blowing me off.

When the convention ended, Jayme and I flew back to Virginia. When I got back, I didn't have the money to invest in that industry. Instead, I went to my brother and told him my vision, asking him to go into business with me to buy those pieces of art. With the next artist show coming up, I knew I had to make it out there to build up my store's name. My brother invested $20K to buy the art. Jayme and I went out to the event, and when the artists saw I was spending money with them, they exchanged contact information with me. This linked me up with other well-known artists in the game. I started building a name for myself in Richmond by bringing in glass art pieces when no one else was.

My brother ended up driving to California with a friend to purchase a new batch of product. They were driving back to Virginia with thirty pounds of weed in the trunk when they got pulled over crossing the border of Texas. He got locked up, but he ended up posting bail by himself and returned to Virginia. At this point, I realized that a lot of cannabis consumers were willing to trade glass pieces for product. This meant I could bring in more profit since the cannabis would sell for more in Virginia than in other states.

Eventually, we saved up enough money to move out of the store and into a townhouse in the suburbs of Richmond. We didn't have enough money to buy furniture, so we bought a single couch we slept on together until I saved up enough money for a bed. Jayme and I went out to another glass convention in Colorado, called the Big Show, along with the first-ever Cannabis Cup. We went and purchased art pieces from various artists and attended the Cannabis Cup afterward. I decided to purchase a batch of edibles that I wanted to send back to Richmond. I told Jayme to mail the product, but she wanted to drive it back instead. To avoid conflict, I agreed.

As we were driving back from Colorado to Richmond with the edibles, a cop profiled us and pulled us over for driving in the left lane for too long in Kansas. The cop searched the car and found the edibles in the trunk. We were both arrested and brought in for interrogation. Due to my immigration status, I knew that if I took the charge, it would put me in the bad graces of immigration since I already had a prior charge. I told the cops that the edibles weren't mine. Jayme did not get the memo and thought I was trying to scapegoat her, so she told the cops the edibles weren't hers either. The cops ended up charging both of us and locked us up. I called up my brother, and he got mad that he would have to post bail for me again. Jayme also called up her family and told them about the situation. At this point, I was more worried for her than myself. I had already been through tougher situations, and this was nothing compared to those. However, it was her first time getting locked up.

The bond was set at $50K each person, which was ridiculous for only $500 worth of edibles. It was difficult for us to post bail, as we weren't locals. My brother had to put his house and a couple of other things on collateral to post my bail. Jayme's father ended up posting her bail. We got the car out of the impound and rented a room for two weeks to wait for our nearby court date. We were like a local Bonnie and Clyde! Everyone saw us on the news, which we had no idea about. This whole experience was a crazy one and unfortunately was one of the hardships we had.

10

STARTING A NEW LIFE WITH JAYME

AFTER OUR COURT DATE, WE drove home, and I took her to a mall and bought her a rose gold ring to ask for her hand in marriage. She agreed, and we sealed the deal in a court marriage. We didn't tell anyone, but her parents found out later through a letter Jayme sent them. Her dad was absolutely devastated, as he wanted to walk his daughter down the aisle and was upset at me. He blamed me for taking away that privilege from him. She didn't want to live with my roommate anymore, so we ended up staying in the store. We lived at the shop for a couple of months, maybe four. It was the two of us and two dogs. We used the Coke machine as a personal fridge. We lived in the loft with air mattresses that the dogs would pop every other day, and my siblings would stay with us sometimes. We learned a lot by living in the store. Since we were at the shop twenty-four seven, I guess we were one up on everyone else, because we were working all the time. All we did was eat, breathe, and work the shop. We worked on being better business owners and worked on inventory, organizing the store, and making it look better.

After saving money, we ended up getting a rental house that was about a twenty-minute walk to the shop, which was very convenient for us.

We had a lot of hardships, and some were traumatic experiences, especially for me. The line of work didn't help either. I always had faith, though, and knew that we would make it out one day.

I went to an immigration lawyer to see if my new marriage would help my immigration status. They told me that their hands were tied because of the two misdemeanor marijuana charges. I felt disappointed and unfortunate because of my immigration status; once again, the system had let me down.

Around this time, my mom and family came to visit me. They stayed with me for a couple days. My mom got a phone call from her sister back in Pakistan, who gave her news she never wanted to hear. The moment she came to the United States, she made it her sole mission to gain citizenship so she could go see her mom again. After twenty-five long years of praying to see her again, my mom learned from her sister that her mom had just passed away. She was devastated beyond words, her dream shattering right before her eyes. She would grieve in pain for the next few months. She became very distant from my siblings and me.

One day, my brother had a shipment of marijuana sent from California. What we didn't know was that the package had already been seized by the DEA. My brother had sent his girlfriend to pick up the package. When she got there, a pink slip was loosely attached to the door, with a message telling her to go to the post office to pick up the package. When she went to the post office, she got pushed into an interrogation room. Two officers were in the room and questioned her about the package. She pleaded that she needed to pick up her son from the bus stop, and when the cops asked where, she made a critical mistake by giving up the house address. Later that day, undercover cops surrounded the entire house.

When my brother stepped out for his daily run with some packs, our little brother knew something was fishy and quickly realized that the house was surrounded by undercover cops. The whole scene looked like a sting operation. He quickly retracted his steps and went back into the house. My little brother had an idea to take the packs out, and my brother had just left to see what was going on. He left the house with the car completely empty, and seconds later, the cops pulled him over and started to search his vehicle. He asked them if they had an arrest warrant or if he was being detained. When the cops answered no, he drove off.

My older brother called my younger brother at home and told him to stay inside and keep quiet if he was questioned. At this point, my younger brother was only a naive little gamer kid who never got out of the house. He was oblivious to the bigger picture. He didn't really know what was going on, and he was scared. When the cops finally got a warrant, they kicked the door in and rushed in with M16-like rifles pointed at his head. Eventually they took my little brother in for questioning. While they were questioning my little brother, they found a quarter million in cash stashed with five pounds of marijuana in an upstairs bedroom. My little brother didn't know better, and the interrogators were asking the questions in such a way they could only be answered with a yes or a no. He ended up unknowingly confessing everything they were asking, which caused him to have a felony on his record. They arrested my little brother and took him to a jail with a small bond. My mom and our family had to go bond him out. Then we went to our townhouse that we had for rent. My brother who got away had a warrant out for his arrest. He ended up hiding at a mutual friend's house until things blew over.

Later that day, I told him to leave Fredericksburg and just come to Richmond because the cops would be looking for him. He came to my house. My two little brothers and my mom were at the house my brother rented for them. The next day, the cops barely knocked on the door, and before my little brother could make it downstairs, they started to break the door down. They were yelling at him, "Open the door!" But the door was already stuck and could not be opened because they jammed the lock.

"The door is stuck. Go ahead and break it open," said my little brother. They put him in handcuffs after they broke the door. They went upstairs to my mom and youngest brother. With assault rifles, they went upstairs where my mom was.

"Get on the ground!" yelled the cops with a gun pointed to her neck. She didn't understand English very well, so she lay facedown on the bed. She eventually understood what they were telling her to do and got on the ground, and they put her in handcuffs. They brought everyone to the main floor to be questioned. They tried asking my mom questions, but my mom just didn't understand, so they got my youngest brother, who was too young to be put in handcuffs at the time.

One of the cops got down on one knee and said, "We know you know the answers." My youngest brother acted like he didn't know anything. They didn't find anything but a bong in a trash can in front of the house. They ended up leaving with the door so busted you couldn't even close it.

Thankfully, we had left right before the cops kicked down the door at my mom's house. My brother ended up staying at my house in Richmond because he wanted to make sure he had a lawyer before he turned himself in. My brother was already on probation due to his Texas run-in with law enforcement. He wasn't allowed to have any new convictions, so we had to wait for his bond hearing. Time was of the essence, and he needed a bond out since his Texas trial was right around the corner.

At the bond hearing, the prosecuting attorney convinced the judge to prevent him from getting a bond out. They made the case around false accusations, saying he had ties to cartels, in order to justify the amount of cash that was found. The judge agreed, not allowing him to post bond. He was stressed, as not making the Texas trial date would put him in a really tough situation. If he didn't make the court date, the state of Texas would find out about his new charges. By the grace of God, the bondsman informed us that my brother already had a bond posted in the system. We ended up bonding him out, allowing him to make his Texas court date. When he returned, the state sent another warrant out for his arrest, not knowing he was posted on bond due to a complication in the system. He faced trial again, and in court, the judge was infuriated, asking why he left if he wasn't supposed to. It was a day to remember, but by the grace of God, this glitch in the system allowed him to make his Texas court date.

To avoid getting a drug charge, which would have negatively affected his immigration status, he ended up forfeiting the quarter million dollars. The system ended up allowing him out on probation. With the small amount of cash we had left, we bought a turnkey location and started another smoke shop. We also bought some land in Clearlake, California, to grow cannabis. My brother hired his friend for $3,000 per month to grow cannabis for us. We sent him all the setup money needed for a proper weed grow. We added the whole nine, a well, irrigation, and so on, all to set up our first successful weed grow. For the first time, everything seemed like it was going well.

One morning, the probation officer called my brother for him to come in. What we didn't know was that ICE was waiting for him at the office. They arrested and detained him for the charges he was facing in Texas. At the time, we had no idea, until my brother's girlfriend called my mom, telling her about the situation. I still remember my mom rushing down the stairs with tears streaming down her face while I sat out in the backyard with my dogs. The next day, it hit us that my brother was facing deportation. The best immigration lawyer wanted $20K to defend my brother. I had to find a way to come up with the money.

During this time, I was also hit with all the bills from our business operations and combined ventures, as well as our family bills. I had a connection who brought pounds in from Michigan, so my friend and I went in on twenty five pounds for $50K. When the batch came in, I made the mistake of not opening the package, assuming the weed was good from what I had seen and past business transactions. The next day when buyers came in, we found out that each gram of weed had around thirty seeds in it. Due to the large number of seeds, the buyers backed out. I called my contact and asked him to make it right. "I need the money for my current circumstances," I pleaded. He responded, "I don't give a fuck. It's not my problem."

At this point, I started losing customers because I didn't have the funds to purchase new product. I sent out my last $7,500 to my contact in California to send me five pounds of product. The package wasn't secure and ended up getting stolen. I felt stuck, in a deep hole that was drowning me. Worst of all, it was a hole that I dug for myself. I had a $1,100 bill due for my mortgage, and when I went to the ATM and deposited my money, the machine said that it was out of service right after I put in my money. Out of rage and frustration, I started kicking the machine. I had to call the bank, and they were able to credit me the amount that wasn't credited. At some point, my family had to move in with me, which Jayme certainly wasn't fond of. But at that time, I had no choice. I was broke and losing my customer base due to the lack of product.

I had a glass art piece I had paid $30K for, which I marketed myself on social media. Eventually, I found a buyer in California who offered me $15K cash and a pound of oil. I had no choice but to take the loss and resell it because I needed the money for my brother's attorney. I ended up mailing the oil back to Virginia from California. I flew back and gave the $15K to my brother's girlfriend, all while waiting for the oil to come in the mail. I resold the oil in smaller batches and was able to make some money off of it, so I was able to get by.

One day, I got a call from a friend asking for a connection to purchase some weed. I informed him that I had people out in California who could get him some good product. I told Jayme that I had to fly out to California to make this transaction possible. I called up my seller and asked her to send me a list of all the strains she had for me to send over to my friend. I informed her to mark up prices $1K per pound. My friend had agreed to shop with my connection, so we flew out to California together. He purchased ten pounds, which meant I was able to turn a $10K profit, which I then used to purchase product myself. We packaged our product and shipped it out.

The next day, we flew back to Virginia. I used this money to pay my overdue bills. With the little money I had left, I told Jayme I had to go out to California to get back on my feet. I flew back to California and was able to rent a car. I had customers, but there were nights I had to sleep in my rental, as I relied on customers to reach out to me. At this point, I could no longer pay my grower at the plantation the $3K per month, so I started looking for investors. I called up a guy who used to host the glass conventions. I offered him a 50 percent stake in the operation to help me get the whole thing set up properly. He agreed and gave me a couple of pounds as payment. I used this to get back on my feet. This guy also gave me free sponsorships for future shows.

At this point, I was still stuck paying the monthly mortgages by myself. At the end of the day, this supposed partner never pulled through on his end of the deal, even though I had already made him 50 percent owner on the deed to the land. Eventually, I was able to save up enough money to get an apartment in Pasadena, which I ran my weed operation out of, packaging and selling packs.

My wife, Jayme, resented selling weed for me in Virginia, as it was illegal. The arrest in Kansas left her with really bad anxiety, to the point where she got really bad panic attacks. Due to this, I had to teach my younger sister the ins and outs of my business. At the very least, I was able to trust my family, and my sister was already conditioned to this life. My sister started handling my side of the business in Virginia. When my brother's trial date came up, his girlfriend, who was a Jew, made the case to the judge, saying he was a convert and that it would be dangerous for him if he got deported. Since Muslims don't like Jews, it would put him in a difficult position. They even had a rabbi make a testimony in court saying he attended the Messianic Temple. This was an elaborate way to ensure my brother's safety and to prevent him from getting deported. In the end, our efforts were fruitful since the judge allowed him to stay in the United States. He was finally free.

11

THE BEGINNING OF THE END

AT THIS POINT, I WAS still living in California, when one day Jayme called me saying she wanted to move out there with me. I was also in search of a bigger location because we had four dogs at that time. When I lived in Pasadena, I was really antisocial and mainly kept to myself, but at some point, I ended up getting a Maltese to blend in with my neighbors. My antisocial tendencies came from my past and when locked up because I really didn't talk to anyone other than my family. This made me incredibly isolated but also redirected my focus toward making money and doing better for myself and my family.

I started attending cannabis events to build my network by finding farmers who had weed for good prices. This way, I could buy products from them to supply my customers who would come into town or for packages I had to ship out. The problem was that the majority of the weed farmers lived in Murrieta, so I had to drive out there on a daily basis to pick up supply. One of the farmers suggested that I move nearby so I wouldn't have to make the daily commute. I came to realize it was a pretty good idea since the houses out there were decently sized and priced. My goal was to have Jayme and our dogs eventually move out there with me.

After my brother came home from ICE, I took a trip back to Virginia. I wanted to check on the smoke shop, and I realized that the FedEx driver whom I had grown close to could possibly give me locations to ship my products to. I offered him $1K per package if this could work. I flew back to California to resume my business there after that was deemed a viable plan. I coordinated for my sister to pick up the packages and then drop them off to the customers. She would send me the money by depositing it into my business account, which would show my business was making good money. It would be the same money that was being recycled by withdrawing and depositing, since depositing the money to my account was the only way I knew to get the money, so it end up costing me way more in taxes at the end of the year.

After returning to California, I quickly secured a property in Murrieta to rent. During this time, Jayme and her dad drove to California with the dogs and all her personal belongings to move in with me. At that time, I was incredibly numb and felt dead inside. Some days, it felt as if all that mattered to me was making money, and I had no care for anything else in the world. I had never been shown love my entire life, which meant that I didn't know how to reciprocate love or show affection. My wife and I were often in conflict, particularly at times throughout our relationship when she came off as controlling. The relationship grew to be incredibly toxic. I learned to distance myself as a way of self-preservation, but it somehow always felt like Jayme wanted to be in competition with me. On the contrary, I'd always looked at us as a team. I wanted both of us to find success.

I remember getting a booth to sell weed at a cannabis event. I met a very knowledgeable person who let me in on the new wave for future business growth in our sector. Many people were buying vape cartridges, and a huge market had opened up. It was the new wave. Due to certain California state laws, I was prohibited from buying vapes from licensed companies. Instead, I began making vape cartridges and selling them myself. I had a really close friend fill them for me. I paid them $1.50 for each cartridge they filled. The vape cartridges had about a $6–$7 production cost per unit, and I sold them for $20 each. This meant I turned over 50 percent profit on each cartridge. However, I started needing help due to the number of orders I was getting on a daily basis, nearly nonstop orders.

One day, I received a call from my old boss, who worked at 7-Eleven as an owner/manager. I still saw him as a friend, regardless of what had happened between us. He proceeded to tell me he had gotten caught cheating again when his wife left home. He was considering moving to California to save the marriage. He wanted to know if there was something he could do to make money. One thing about me, I will put people on. If I know how to do something or have a vision that I prospered from, I'll show you. If I have what you need, I'll give it to you. I replied, "Yeah, just come out. I got you," without even consulting with my wife. Later on, I asked my wife if it was OK for him and his family to move there for little bit so I could help them. She strongly disagreed because she liked her privacy. It took some work, but I finally convinced her, and I told him he could come out and help fill vape cartridges. He moved into our house with his wife and his kids, and I was never the guy who cared about money, so I didn't ask him for rent or anything. Every time we went out or ate, I paid for everyone.

The vape orders kept growing, and I sold vape cartridges in bulk to certain clients. I didn't see much profit selling them in bulk amounts of 10K+ locally, but I had buyers coming out of town to buy them, which I made huge margins on. During this time, I saved up a decent sum of money from all the cartridge sales. I decided to purchase a property in Murrieta, putting $100K down. At the same time, I helped my brother buy a house in Virginia, putting $225K down.

I started looking into breeding dogs. I told my friend about the big breeders in the game and showed him the vision of how much money they were bringing in. I told him we could do the same thing, and we both invested in extra-large pit bulls for the breeding program. Then I saw how much money the French bulldogs were bringing in and told him we should look into them as well. Throughout my life, I've always liked having multiple sources of income so I can reach success quicker, so we bought some French bulldogs for our program as well.

My ex-7-Eleven boss saved up money from his stores and helping me make cartridges and decided to buy a house in Palm Springs, and my wife and I moved to our new house. I had to keep the rental to keep the production going, but then, out of nowhere, the pen market started crashing. People started making cheaper-quality pens and selling them for cheap. Even though my quality was way better, the majority of consumers preferred to buy something cheap than something that was quality. I had spent close to $100K in new inventory, which was now just sitting.

Then I got a call from my friend, saying that he needed to sell his house due to his financial situation. He asked if he could move in and said he would pay me $1,500 toward my $2,500 rent. I agreed, so they moved in there. He never paid me rent, nor did I ever ask. Jayme and I got super close to our neighbors at the time. They would come over and hang out, have cookouts, and so on. They woke up to us arguing the majority of the time, and everyone we knew always told us, "You guys are too toxic for each other. You guys can't live like this. It is not healthy."

My friend and his family would always come over, and we would chill and play spades. He would sometimes say things like, "Your neighbor is pretty toned up," because she worked out and was toned for her age. We talked like men usually talk, and he told me how he would fuck the hell out of her and then asked me if I would. I answered, "Yeah, I would too."

Since my vape pen market crashed, I wasn't bringing in the money like I had been before, so it was hard to keep up with the bills. I didn't want to ask my friend, because he never offered to pay me the monthly rent even though he said before he moved in that he would pay me $1,500 per month. My mailing packs through the organized FedEx way crashed right after that. I sent out around ten boxes throughout the week by sending two boxes per day, and every single one of the boxes got seized by the postal inspectors. This caused us a huge loss.

12

THE FINAL NAIL IN
THE COFFIN

I HAD AROUND $50K SAVED up at this time. I had been doing business with an Asian lady for a couple of years, selling packs and stuff in LA to buyers together. She ran a health care business and told me she could help me make money if I wanted to invest in her company. Not having any other sources of income, I ended up agreeing to invest with her and gave her the $50K. She promised me a certain amount of money back. Then, out of nowhere, she disappeared on me with my money. Her phone stopped working, so I was like, "Fuck, I literally got robbed by someone I thought I knew!"

I really started stressing about my bills, and then at some point, there was a huge drought that killed most of the weed supply that my and other businesses relied on. Someone came to me with low packs, and I realized this could be a new source of income. I would buy them for $300 per pack and resell them for $700 each. Moving thousands of these packs, I was once again able to save up a decent sum of money, with my birthday right around the corner.

I had always told myself that I would buy myself a nice car, so on my birthday, I drove to the exotic car dealership. I asked the salesman what I needed to purchase a 2020 Lamborghini Evo, and he told me to come in with a $100K down payment to finance my desired car. When I told Jayme about this, she strongly discouraged me from going through with the car. On the way to the dealership, she was yelling at me to save the money so we could start a family instead. But I knew I didn't want to bring any kids into this world with Jayme, knowing how toxic our relationship was. I didn't want an innocent kid to have to deal with the consequences of our problems. That day, I walked into the dealership with $100K and walked out with the keys to my dream car. I knew the car would prove to be an investment tool that would open up new opportunities and networks for me. Although Jayme was unhappy, I already had my heart set on it, and no one was going to change my mind.

The low packs market also crashed right after that. Luckily, I had some money saved to buy packs, and I ended up linking up with people in LA to sell packs to out-of-towners to keep up with bills. I had to go to LA just to have a source of income flowing. While I was in LA, my wife told me, "Your friend hit me up, wanting to come smoke with me while you're not here." I didn't think anything of it because he was my friend.

One day, we were having a cookout, and my friend (my ex-boss from 7-Eleven) came over with his wife and kids. My neighbor wanted to check out the Lamborghini, so I took her on a drive. While I was gone, my friend told my wife he wanted to smoke, so they went to the laundry room. He closed the door behind him and told her, while touching her stomach, "You're really attractive to me."

My wife freaked out and said, "You're supposed to be my husband's friend!" He realized she didn't feel what he did, and he told her he was just joking.

When I got home, we were all chilling, but once everyone left, my wife told me what had happened. I got mad and texted him, "You're lucky I have some respect for you, or I would knock you the fuck out." He assumed Jayme was going to tell his wife next, so to save his marriage, he told his wife the reason he did what he did was so I could know the feeling of messing with the neighbor's wife. They both waited until I left to tell Jayme he did it to teach me a lesson. I got home to Jayme crying, spazzing out on me, telling me how I was wrong. I explained myself, but I parted ways with them for peace on both sides. My relationship was already going downhill. This was just the cherry on top. That's just some shit that's out of line. You don't do that to your best friend's wife, no matter what, especially after all I had done for him. I never would've done that to his wife if the tables were turned, out of respect.

13

A TURNING POINT

I STARTED GOING TO CAR events and networking with other exotic car owners. There were a couple of people I got close to, and we quickly became good friends. One day, a friend asked me to do a photoshoot with the car. I told him I was not the most social person and wouldn't exactly branch out to other people unless they came up to me. Considering I'm an intimidating, asshole-looking person, not a lot of people usually come up to me. Nevertheless, I agreed to go, and at the photoshoot, I exchanged Instagrams with a girl named Oryna. There was just something about her that caught my attention right away.

Around this same time, I wanted to get my car wrapped. I had a flashy, chrome, color-changing flower of life design in mind, something different that nobody had seen. I went to RDBLA in Los Angeles and spent $30K to make my car the greatest car out there. The same day it came out, it broke the internet. Every block I drove it down, everyone was pulling out their cameras to take pictures. Kids, adults, and police couldn't help but smile and enjoy the build. It was different. It had so many people talking about the car in the local car community I had to put on a show just for my reveal that same day. Over five thousand car enthusiasts who were curious came from all over San Diego, Los Angeles, and Orange County. They weren't disappointed. Everyone surrounded my car and ignored the other super cars since they'd seen the same thing over and over. The wrap I'd created was one in a million. People still bring it up to this day. The host, Moises, said that it was the most marvelous car that had ever rolled up and the biggest gathering in California in 2020. By the biggest, I mean these guys threw events like no other. People from all of Southern California showed up, and the night was like a movie. People came up to me asking questions left and right, and I felt bad because I couldn't get to everyone since the gathering lasted only two hours. The car has kept gaining popularity ever since. Some people started hating due to all the attention my car was getting. They started getting similar chrome-style wraps for their cars without the design my car had, just so they could take some of the attention off my car.

When Jayme and I attended our first car rally, I was able to network and eventually meet people in the same industry as me. I saw this girl Oryna here and there at the rally, and I decided to shoot her a DM on Instagram because I remembered her telling me she wanted to open a dog-training business. Being an avid dog lover myself, we had mutual interests right off the bat.

One day, I came across a group of people I met in the car scene. One of the people who stood out was a guy named Tashir. Over the course of the next few months, we became close friends. We hung out every day and pulled pranks on each other. We would go to Vegas on a whim and travel elsewhere. Due to how we both managed to have a lot of free time, we became close rather quickly. It started affecting his relationship with his girl. He was around me more than his own girl, who ended up making him go to counseling.

Over the months, as our friend circle grew, Tashir and I, along with some other friends, started to hang out more and go to more events. They were an important part of my life and helped shape the next few months. They helped me become more social and understand friendship, and they supported me through some difficult times. I would always go to my close friends for advice and just to talk about my day. This was a new feeling for me, and I was experiencing it for the first time in thirty-three years.

While I normally hate traveling, a group of us headed out to Austin, Texas, for Tashir's birthday. It was one of my first trips that I took that wasn't for business, a true vacation. While in Austin, we managed to do a host of fun activities like boating, go-karts, and going out at night. I was finally able to let loose one night and take a couple of shots. We might have all gotten too drunk because almost everyone missed their flight the next morning.

Some other trips we took created the best memories for me. I remember taking a weeklong trip to Vegas to buy a monkey. While we were originally supposed to take a road trip to Houston, five hours into the trip, we realized that maybe driving there and back wasn't the best idea. Somewhere past Phoenix, we decided to reroute to Vegas and wait there for the monkey to be delivered. A day or two later, we finally got the monkey and immediately realized that it was way crazier than we had been told. Locked in a hotel room, we let the monkey loose, and it bit my hand. It also smelled terrible, and we couldn't get it to sit still enough to bathe it. The next day, we took it to a monkey trainer and left it there for two weeks to get trained. We never went back for the monkey.

After so much darkness, I was finally having fun with life, and my worries started to fade the more time I spent with my new friends. However, there was still a social aspect of me that had a hard time letting everyone in. During a couple exotic car events that took us to different cities, I took the opportunity to mingle and network with other supercar owners, but I was weary of most of them. It was hard to open up or even communicate because I felt that I didn't have much in common with a lot of people. One of the owners of the rally mentioned that they didn't really need me to come. All I did was talk to the same three to four people every event, and therefore I wasn't really a benefit to the event. I didn't care about the event or give two fucks if I went or not. I was heated about that statement, but I slowly got over it because I realized that Tashir and others stood up for me and fought to have me around. It meant a lot to me and showed me that I finally had a group of true friends.

A few of us started hanging out every day religiously, including Oryna. There was just something about her that kept attracting me to her even though we didn't know each other very well at that time. There was one day when my car had broken down and I hitched a Lyft back home. The entire ride back, she stayed on the phone with me, and I could not comprehend why she cared about me, especially considering we weren't even close at that point. The care that she showed me was something I had never experienced from anyone my entire life. This girl made me feel a sense of safety, especially considering how things at home with Jayme were still so toxic. Some days, I wouldn't even go home because of how bad our relationship had gotten. I never ended up telling Jayme about Oryna because I wanted to continue to get to know her better.

Then we all went to a rally, and Oryna ended up finding out that I was married. Through all that, the sense of security and safety I felt from her kept me attracted to her. She was always there for me, especially when I needed her. I came to realize that our lives were pretty similar. She was essentially a spitting image of me. I came to find out that she was actually my twin flame, essentially a female version of me. I felt like she filled in for what I was lacking and vice versa. This was around the time my wife started hanging out with another guy. They ended up going to a car rally together, but at that point, our relationship was so dead and toxic that I really didn't mind. I hadn't felt the care and love from her that Oryna was able to offer me. It felt like we had known each other for ages. At some point, Jayme and I were going through the process of divorce while Oryna and I were growing closer. She helped me on my darkest days and was always there to lend a hand with my business ventures.

I decided to invest nearly $200K in a weed grow with a couple of partners I did not know particularly well. It sounded like a good opportunity that would yield healthy profits. With the partners' promise of seven hundred to one thousand pounds of weed, I decided to go in on it with the help of Oryna. The support she gave me was unconditional, and she made me feel a type of way that was almost unexplainable. I adored her and loved having her around. I began randomly buying her things. As I did not know how to show affection, that was always my love language. With Jayme and I separated, I sold the house in Murrieta as well as the Lamborghini as a result of the divorce. Around this time, I also bought one hundred pounds of marijuana with my brother to send back to Virginia.

With the help of some friends, I moved out to Irvine, California, while Jayme moved in with the guy she had gone to the rally with. As Oryna and I got busier, it slowly got harder for us to make time for each other. During this time, I took co-ownership in a French bulldog for $40K, with the means to breed her. Oryna helped me watch her while the Frenchie was pregnant, and this caused us to see each other less and less. I had just gotten out of an extremely toxic relationship and was in a bad emotional state. One day, I got mad at Oryna for not making time for me or us. It came from a place of frustration and trauma from my last relationship, but I ended up telling her I was done, even though I didn't mean it. Regardless, it hurt her feelings, and just like that, she put her guard back up. Little did I know, that was not the only foreseeable trouble in my future.

My life would soon make a one-eighty. The weed grow that I had invested a large sum of money into failed, which resulted in me taking a huge loss, while the one hundred pounds of weed I bought with my brother ended up having mold in it. On top of that, the guy I co-owned the French bulldog with played me. He had promised to help me sell the puppies once they were born, and we would split the profit. Once the puppies were born, though, he only wanted his four, leaving me to figure what to do with the other four. I didn't have buyers for these dogs like he did, and he left me high and dry. I had promised Oryna this would be an opportunity for us to make good money, and she had quit her job. Once the plan backfired, Oryna was stuck with eight puppies along with their mother and no income.

Eventually, I bought twenty pounds of indoor weed for $40K. During this time, I lost all motivation, and the marijuana just sat in my house for two months. I had no idea what else to do other than sell weed. It was all I had ever known to make money.

14

A LIGHT IN THE DARKNESS

I ENDED UP TAKING THE last bit of weed I had to New York, in an attempt to move the product out there. When I was in New York, I started looking into spiritual cleanses because I wanted to understand why it seemed as if my life had made a complete one-eighty.

I met a lady, Deidre Pujols, through the car rallies. She seemed to see something in me and wanted to get to know me. We had lunch one day, and I told her my story. Although she didn't hear the whole thing, she seemed pretty shocked. She told me that the reason I was selling marijuana was because it was all I knew. She told me to look deeper for my purpose and why I am here today. She also told me that I needed to do what I love naturally to attract money, and what I love doing is helping people.

I began to reflect on my past and found solace in the fact that I was still standing even after all I had been through. What Deidre told me stuck in my head, so I stayed in New York for three weeks in search of answers. I felt so lost, trying to find myself, but I couldn't find my way out of the dark. Even worse for me was that I couldn't keep Oryna from the dark either. She needed money, but I couldn't help her. I had hit rock bottom financially.

The funny thing was I didn't even care about the money anymore. Since meeting Oryna, my outlook on life had changed. She had been a light in my darkness, giving me the love I never knew I was missing. The feeling I got from her was worth more than anything money could buy, and no amount of money could replace it.

I spent my days just walking around by the water, and I started getting signs from the universe to write this book. I saw many things that were too big to be coincidences, and I started having vivid dreams about writing the book. My brother had a dream about it as well, where he was coming to see me, but he couldn't get to me because I was signing books and the line was too long.

I ultimately decided to write a book about my life, thinking perhaps it could serve as the light to someone's darkness.

Now you might be wondering why someone like me would think they could be a light, seeing as I was so broken. And you are right. Someone raised with love and care and direction views and navigates the world differently from someone raised on his own by surviving. However, before you judge me, what would you have done in my shoes, with the cards I was dealt?

The way I see it, this was a turning point for me. I could have grown up and chosen to be just like my dad and my grandfather, choosing violence and perpetuating the cycle. But I have chosen to break the chains.

I never let the money change me, though I saw it change others. I could have been greedy and gotten involved in drugs other than marijuana, but I didn't. Subconsciously, I felt it was bad karma—the other drugs can kill people.

Life knocked me down so many times, until pain wasn't painful anymore. Through the thirty-three years of my life, I never felt the love and care I craved. I was so dark and numb and had been dead on the inside for so long. If it didn't make me money, I didn't care about it. I basically had everything—the money, the cars—and was able to scratch everything on my bucket list, but I was still empty inside.

That only changed after I met my car show friends and Oryna. They taught me love by caring about me, and they helped me realize what I was missing throughout my whole life. I'd trade all the money in the world to have that caring, loving feeling.

I tried to give my brothers and sister the life I didn't have by being there for them. I know what it is like when nobody is there for you. We never told each other, "I love you," or, "I care about you." My mom cared about us, but she was never able to give the love and affection a kid deserves. Her whole life was wasted living in fear and getting abused.

Of course, I wonder how my life might have turned out differently. What if my mom had stepped up to the plate when I told social services we were being abused? What if my mom had had a voice and had not had to marry my dad in the first place? Would we have had a loving family instead? What if my dad had just put down his fists and learned to be a better father? Where would my family be right now?

Most of all, I wonder what I ever did to deserve this.

But I don't wallow in self-pity for choices that weren't made. Instead, I am grateful for the experiences I have had. I forgive my mother, my father, and my grandfather for their choices, and I know that what I have been through because of them has only made me stronger.

Throughout my experiences, I realized that success isn't about how much money you have; it's about the difference you make in people's lives. I feel my purpose in life is to help others. I want to be the motivation for other people and make this world a better place. I want to be an inspiration for the weak who can't stand up for themselves, women and children suffering abuse.

I want to show the world that no matter how bad life beat me down, I still managed to get back up. No matter how badly

I wanted to give up, hope whispered, "Just keep going." The same goes for you.

Life is all about the choices you make, and each choice comes with consequences. Nothing is free in this world. Every choice you make comes with a price you have to pay, so why not make the right choice now, so you don't have to pay the price later?

Only dead fish go with the flow. Become your higher self, so you can fearlessly harness the power of going against the flow, no matter what circumstances you're put in. Never give up, and keep pushing. Eventually, you will see the light.

My mom never missed a prayer a day of her life, but because she took no action, nothing changed. That is not to say prayers aren't good, but if there is one thing I've learned from all of this, it is that you are the only one who can take action to change your life. Don't wait on someone else to do it, or it will never happen.

Just keep going. It does get better.

Made in the USA
Middletown, DE
16 October 2023

40941186R00076